PERSPECTIVES ON SUPERVISION

Other titles in the

Systemic Thinking and Practice Series

edited by David Campbell and Ros Draper
published and distributed by Karnac

Asen, E., Dawson N. & McHugh B. *Multiple Family Therapy: The Marlborough Model and its Wider Applications*
Bentovim, A. *Trauma-Organized Systems: Physical and Sexual Abuse in Families*
Boscolo, L. & Bertrando, P. *Systemic Therapy with Individuals*
Burck, C. & Daniel, G. *Gender and Family Therapy*
Campbell, D., Draper, R. & Huffington, C. *Second Thoughts on the Theory and Practice of the Milan Approach to Family Therapy*
Campbell, D., Draper, R. & Huffington, C. *Teaching Systemic Thinking*
Campbell, D. & Mason, B. (Eds) *Perspectives on Supervision*
Cecchin, G., Lane, G.& Ray, W. A. *The Cybernetics of Prejudices in the Practice of Psychotherapy*
Cecchin, G., Lane, G. & Ray, W.A. *Irreverence: A Strategy for Therapists Survival*
Dallos, R. *Interacting Stories: Narratives, Family Beliefs and Therapy*
Draper, R., Gower, M. & Huffington, C. *Teaching Family Therapy*
Farmer, C. *Psychodrama and Systemic Therapy*
Flaskas, C. & Perlesz, A. (Eds) *The Therapeutic Relationship in Systemic Therapy*
Fredman, G. *Death Talk: Conversations with Children and Families*
Hildebrand, J. *Bridging the Gap: A Training Module in Personal and Professional Development*
Hoffman, L. *Exchanging Voices: A Collaborative Approach to Family Therapy*
Johnsen, A., Sundet, R., & Wie Tortsteinsson, V. *Self in Relationships: Perspectives on Family Therapy from Developmental Psychology*
Jones, E. *Working with Adult Survivors of Child Sexual Abuse*
Jones, E. & Asen, E. *Systemic Couple Therapy and Depression*
Krause, I.-B. *Culture and System in Family Therapy*
Mason, B. & Sawyerr, A. (Eds) *Exploring the Unsaid: Creativity, Risks and Dilemmas in Working Cross-Culturally*
Robinson, M *Divorce as Family Transition: When Private Sorrow Becomes a Public Matter*
Smith, G. *Systemic Approaches to Training in Child Protection*
Wilson, J. *Child-Focused Practice: A Collaborative Systemic Approach*

Work with Organisations

Campbell, D *The Socially Constructed Organization*
Campbell, D. *Learning Consultation: A Systemic Framework*
Campbell, D. *The Socially Constructed Organization*
Campbell, D., Coldicott, T. & Kinsella, K. *Systemic Work with Organizations: A New Model for Managers and Change Agents*
Campbell, D, Draper, R. & Huffington, C *A Systemic Approach to Consultation*
Cooklin, A. (Ed) *Changing Organizations: Clinicians as Agents of Change*
Haslebo, G. & Nielsen, K.S. *Systems and Meaning: Consulting in Organizations*
Huffington, C. & Brunning, H. (Eds) *Internal Consultancy in the Public Sector: Case Studies*
Huffington, C., Cole, C., Brunning, H. *A Manual of Organizational Development: The Psychology of Change*
McCaughan, N. & Palmer, B. *Systems Thinking for Harassed Managers*

PERSPECTIVES ON SUPERVISION

Edited by

David Campbell & Barry Mason

Foreword by

Gill Gorell Barnes

Systemic Thinking and Practice Series

Series Editors

David Campbell & Ros Draper

First published in 2002 by
H. Karnac (Books) Ltd.
6 Pembroke Buildings, London NW10 6RE

Reprinted 2003, 2005

British Library Cataloguing in Publication Data

A C.I.P. for this book is available from the British Library

ISBN 1 85575 280 8

10 9 8 7 6 5 4 3

Edited, designed, and produced by Communication Crafts

Printed in Great Britain

www.karnacbooks.com

CONTENTS

SERIES EDITORS' FOREWORD

The development of the profession of psychotherapy, including family therapy, both in Europe and in the United States, has followed a predictable course. It began by accrediting therapists and training courses and, as the field matured, moved on to supervisors and their training standards. In the United Kingdom, the national register for family therapy supervisors has been up and running for several years, but the attempts to theorize and understand the supervision process have lagged behind the administrative activity. This book fills some of that void. It has a singular focus on supervision, with a range of contributions that are united by their commitment to explaining the theories that underpin the practices of supervision.

David Campbell and Barry Mason are experienced supervisors in the family therapy field in the United Kingdom. On behalf of their respective institutions, the Tavistock Clinic and the Institute of Family Therapy in London, they recently organized a joint conference on the subject of supervision from the systemic perspective. The international contributors to this volume represent four different countries and present models of supervision that have been adapted to suit particular contexts, such as child protection, eating disorders, work with refugees, working across cultures and theoretical models, and the context of training for both family therapy and family therapy supervision.

This is certainly a book for supervisors, regardless of their theoretical persuasion, but it is more than that. Being also an exciting advancement of systemic thinking, it is of interest for any systemic practitioner. Because supervision is hierarchical, a supervisor has to incorporate notions of power with her or his notion of co-constructed realities. The contributors to this volume have not shirked from such challenges, and the reader will find the chapters fresh and stimulating.

David Campbell
Ros Draper
London, 2002

ABOUT THE AUTHORS

The Editors

David Campbell is a consultant clinical psychologist working at the Tavistock Clinic, London, and as a freelance consultant to organizations. He has been involved in organizing and supervising on family therapy training courses since their inception in 1975. He is also a founder member of the Institute of Family Therapy, a past supervisor, and a current member of council.

Barry Mason is the Director of the Institute of Family Therapy. He has been involved in the training of systemic therapists and practitioners since 1983 as well as in developing post-qualifying training programmes in supervision and co-developing criteria for the registration of supervisors and supervision courses in the U.K.

The Contributors

Margaret Bennett is a systemic family psychotherapist in a child and adolescent mental health service (CAMHS), a child supervisor and teacher on the qualifying Family Therapy Diploma Course at the Prudence Skynner Family Therapy Clinic, and a freelance supervisor and systemic family psychotherapist in private practice and at Kingston Gate Therapy Service.

Charlotte Burck is the organising tutor of the Family Therapy Supervision Course at the Tavistock Clinic, London, where she works as a family therapist, a trainer, and a researcher.

John Burnham is Consultant Family Therapist, Parkview Clinic, Birmingham Children's Hospital NHS Trust, and Director of Training in Systemic Teaching, Training and Supervision, KCC, London.

Jeff Faris is a Senior Lecturer at the Family Institute, School of Care Sciences, University of Glamorgan, Wales.

Laura Fruggeri is a Professor at the Department of Psychology, University of Parma, and Senior Faculty Member at the Centro Milanese di Terapia della Famiglia. She has done extensive research into the analysis of the therapeutic processes and has published several articles and books in this area.

Myrna Gower is an individual, couple, and family psychotherapist and is also a freelance systemic supervisor and teacher. She is Associate Lecturer, Royal Holloway, University of London.

Vivienne Gross is a family therapist and supervisor at South West London and St George's NHS Mental Health Trust, Child and Adolescent Eating Disorders Service, and the Prudence Skynner Family Therapy Clinic. She is also a part-time personal/professional development tutor on the MSc. course in Family and Systemic Psychotherapy at the Institute of Family Therapy, London.

Queenie Harris is a consultant child and family psychiatrist and co-director of the family therapy training programme at Parkview Clinic, Birmingham.

Cynthia Maynerd is Head of Family Therapy, CAMHS, South West London and St George's Mental Health NHS Trust and a supervisor at the Prudence Skynner Family Therapy Clinic.

Jørn Nielsen is a clinical psychologist in private practice. He is also a part-time lecturer in clinical psychology at the Danish University of Education (Danmarks Pædagogiske Universitet).

Renos K. Papadopoulos is a professor at the University of Essex, a consultant clinical psychologist at the Tavistock Clinic, a family systems psychotherapist, and a training and supervising Jungian analyst. At the Tavistock, he has been involved with refugee work for many years, working clinically with families and supervising, consulting, and teaching specialist courses. As consultant to the United Nations and other organizations, he has worked with survivors of violence and disaster in several countries.

Valeria Pomini, a clinical psychologist and psychotherapist, trained at the Milan Centre for Family Therapy in the 1980s and now works as a clinician, researcher, and supervisor at the Family Therapy Unit and the Outpatient Clinic for Drug and Alcohol Addiction, Eginition Hospital, University of Athens. She is co-director of the training course in Systemic and Marital Therapy at the University of Athens Mental Health Research Institute.

Vlassis Tomaras is Associate Professor of Psychiatry at the University of Athens. He is also Chair of the Family Therapy Unit, Eginition Hospital, University of Athens, and co-director of the training course in Systemic and Marital Therapy at the University of Athens Mental Health Research Institute.

Gill Wyse is a systemic family psychotherapist in a child and adolescent mental health service (CAMHS) and in a private eating-disorder clinic, a supervisor and teacher on the qualifying Family Therapy Diploma Course at the Prudence Skynner Family Therapy Clinic, and a freelance teacher, supervisor, and therapist in private practice.

About the Institutions

The Tavistock Clinic is a large NHS training centre for post-graduate psychotherapy training, as well as a local child and adult mental health clinic. Established in 1920 using psychoanalytic models of individual and group therapy, in 1975 it also became the home of the first family-therapy training course in the U.K. and now has a thriving group of systemic therapists who staff family therapy and systemic courses from introductory to doctoral level, including the course in family therapy training described in this volume.

The Institute of Family Therapy (IFT) was founded in 1977 under its first Chair of Council, the late Dr Robin Skynner. Over the last 25 years it has become well known for its training courses (from introductory to doctoral level) and its clinical work, including its mediation service. It has a membership of nearly 200 senior practitioners based all over the U.K. and beyond. The Institute has always sought to initiate new developments in response to emerging needs, and in this respect it has recently established the Centre for Child Focused Practice. The President of the Institute is Yasmin Alibhai-Brown, MBE.

Further information about the Tavistock Clinic and the Institute of Family Therapy can be obtained from:

The Tavistock Clinic
120 Belsize Lane
London NW3 5BA

tel: 44 (0) 20 7435 7111
fax: 44 (0) 20 7447 3733
email: childandfamily@tavi-port.demon.co.uk
web page: www.tavi-port.org

The Institute of Family Therapy
24–32 Stephenson Way
London NW1 2HX

tel: 44 (0)20 7391 9150
fax: 44 (0)20 7391 9169
email: ift@psyc.bbk.ac.uk
web page: www.instituteoffamilytherapy.org.uk

FOREWORD

Gill Gorell Barnes

Formerly Consultant for Training, the Institute of Family Therapy, and Honorary Senior Lecturer, the Tavistock Clinic

This is a good book, by good people, about good practices. It is a book reflecting postmodern practice. Certain words and themes recur throughout: transparency, reflexivity, collaborative, sensitive. These words are anchored in the practices described in the text, and these in turn all stem from ongoing clinical work. One of the strengths of the book, itself very varied in content, is that all the practitioners are just that—regular, ongoing "postmodern" practitioners: clinicians within social and health-care delivery contexts in which they hold themselves accountable at levels of clinical practice, supervision, and teaching. Theory is rarely far from the work itself.

Why am I writing the foreword to this book? I believe that it is in my honorary role as "training elder" in the supervision field. Another recent book on supervision, *Systemic Supervision: A Portable Model for Supervision Training*, which I co-authored in 2000 with Gwynneth Down and Damian McCann, arose from our experience of developing a supervision training together in the early 1990s at the Institute of Family Therapy, a training that would "fit" with the requirements of the Association of Family Therapy as they developed standards. Much of the content in that book reflected the excitement of developing frameworks for assessing aspects of practice and the necessary lenses for scrutinizing the self of the therapist, including ethnicity, gender, and sexuality.

This present book shows the "state of the art"—the developed strength of systemic supervision. It also contains the eclecticism and individuality that happily continue to characterize good systemic practice. The book has a wide framework and a more centred postmodern perspective. It arises from a conference in which a number of people who had not formerly worked regularly together presented their work on supervision within different settings, including some from European countries (Fruggeri, Tamaras & Pomini, Faris, Nielsen). It reflects more firmly the move into the paradigm shift of a second-order perspective and the implications that this has had for the development of practice and training—for example, the use of feedback at all levels of the training and therapeutic system, openness of recorded process (e.g. in the recording devices suggested by Mason), openness of training for supervision practices (Burck & Campbell), or openness of ongoing clinical governance through self-monitoring and ongoing reflective processes (Bennett & colleagues). Overall, the concepts of feedback, openness, multifaceted perspectives, and relational processes—whether in Athens, Birmingham, Cardiff, Denmark, London, Milan, or the South of England—characterize the practice throughout. The developmental struggles of supervision as an activity with its own vocabulary, philosophy, and skills encompass also the ongoing tensions between hierarchy—the structures and clinical accountability required by management within different services, with models for collaborative, co-constructed supervisory practice and training—and these issues are also addressed here.

The first part of the book contains two chapters, one by Laura Fruggeri and one by John Burnham and Queenie Harris. Fruggeri opens with a brilliant analysis of the interplay between constructivist and constructionist perspectives as she sees these in relation to different levels of description in the therapeutic and supervisory process. She dances like a laser beam between concepts and contexts involved in therapeutic systems, in thinking and teaching about them, and in their supervision. Burnham and

Harris show an equal versatility in bringing multiple perspectives to the supervisory process, introducing the acronym of the SOCIAL GRRAACCES (gender, race, religion, age ability, class, culture, ethnicity, sexuality) to the therapeutic and supervisory process—perspectives that may be foreground or background at different times. Each of the first two chapters, therefore, draws attention to multiple perspectives, to a range of positions, and to different levels in thinking about context within therapeutic and supervisory processes.

The second part focuses on perspectives on training, the details of "training for supervision" emerging from four different courses. Barry Mason elucidates a reflective recording format for supervisors and trainees that is designed to help trainees improve their abilities to elicit themes from content and to explore them through time, across relationships, and across contexts while adhering to a central systemic notion that therapy is concerned with trying to explore different perceptions of reality. Charlotte Burck and David Campbell analyse a multi-layered learning system in which the level of the supervisor–therapist relationship is the primary focus of the trainer. This is examined across a number of different contexts, and feedback from the trainee supervisors on the experiences of "training in supervision" forms a central part of the learning process for the trainers as well as for the supervisors in training. Vlassis Tomaras and Valeria Pomini describe changing models for supervision in their Athens training, further emphasizing the openness of the process in which they have experimented with different models for live supervision of supervisors, as well as obtaining trainee feedback through questionnaires throughout the process. Like Burnham and Harris, they raise important questions about recognizing differences in the needs and expectations of supervisees: Burnham and Harris in relation to the cultural context from which a supervisor-in-training may come and/or may subsequently go to practice, and Tamaras and Pomini in relation to the working context, whether therapeutic or managerial, which may require different applications of learning. These suggest the need for reflections on the suitability and idiosyncrasies of the application of "generic" ideas to the specificities of different "practices" as an important component of the development of training itself. Jeff Faris, reflecting on process and personal development, then provides a fascinating narrative of one Buddhist perspective in relation to potential personal development of self, and he describes some of the ways he has developed this within the training setting: "In the light of the necessity and inevitability of discourses of professionalization, evidence-based practice, government initiatives on quality assurance of training courses, and occupational standards for psychotherapy and supervision, I often need to highlight for myself the personhood of trainees, ourselves as teachers and supervisors, and our relationship to these large-system discourses."

The third part, on perspectives on practice, places a tighter emphasis on grounding theories around supervising in contexts of clinical experience and the specific issues involved, including the dilemmas of authority, responsibility, and accountability. Vivienne Gross provides a vivid and meticulous account of training in a setting where life and death are daily issues, detailing clinical vignettes that exactly complement the supervisory dilemmas she is describing: "The transposing of collaborative, co-constructed, non-didactic, and conversational approaches to family therapy supervision into the context of inpatient treatment services for child and adolescent eating disorders, where the life-threatening nature of the primary problem cannot be overlooked, poses unique tensions." Jørn Nielsen describes the challenge for supervision in work with families where the urge towards social control poses a constant challenge to the therapeutic intent, providing, through what he has named a "dialogic arena," a place where each of these facets of work and its potential outcome can be deconstructed and discussed. He places an important emphasis on "doubt" as an ongoing element of this work and the need for this doubt to have a contextual frame in which it can be verbalized, examined, and elaborated upon. He brings in the important issue of legal and political voices, often ignored in therapy, as discourses at a wider level contributing to doubt at an individual level that often need to be addressed as one of the specificities where issues of social control are involved. The third contribution, by Renos Papadopoulos, is less to do with supervision than a *tour de force* on the subject of therapeutic work with refugees, in which he uses one case example to illustrate much larger issues relating to the lenses used for the "treatment" of refugees in this country.

Papadopoulos argues that the "trauma narrative" that characterizes refugee work is privileged above other descriptions that might give rise to other thoughts and conversations, joining refugees to other kinds of family work rather than, as he believes is happening now, separating refugee work into a special category.

The final part, co-authored by Margaret Bennett, Myrna Gower, Cynthia Maynerd, and Gill Wyse, offers a model for clinical governance: self-evaluation of performance, modification of goals in the light of feedback, clinical audit, self-regulation by professionals of themselves. It sets out models of transparency in the practice of self-monitoring "that we believe we expect from those whom we teach and to whom we consult". It is a clear and valuable model of how practice may be developed and opened up at every level, including the audit of supervision itself.

The reader will find that there is much in this book to excite thought and strengthen further frameworks for the professional development of systemic practice and supervision.

INTRODUCTION

In March 1999, the Institute of Family Therapy and the Tavistock Clinic in London collaborated in presenting a conference called "Systemic Supervision: Developments in Practice". We realized that although there had been many conferences held over the years on aspects of systemic therapy and practice, no conference addressing developments in supervision had been held in the United Kingdom since a 1981 conference at the Tavistock, which resulted in the publication of a book edited by John Byng-Hall and Rosemary Whiffen (1982). Similarly, this book has arisen out of the 1999 conference.

Over the past ten years, supervision has begun to take a more central place in systemic therapy theory and practice. Part of this, in the U.K. at least, has been due, we believe, to the growing popularity in family therapy training at an advanced level. The development of these courses required clinical supervisors, and the Association for Family Therapy and Systemic Practice in the U.K. recognized this when, in the early 1990s, it established a group to devise criteria for the registration of supervisors in family therapy and courses in the training of family therapy supervisors. This initiative resulted in the publication of *The Red Book* (Burnham, Daniel, Draper, & Mason, 1996).

Systemic supervision and consultation have developed considerably in the last twenty years. Developments have been influenced by the major paradigm shift in the 1980s from a first-order to second-order perspective (Hoffman, 1985) and the implications that this has had for practice and the nature of the therapeutic relationship. Newer therapeutic models have developed, such as solution-focused approaches and narrative approaches as well as an increasing emphasis on collaborative perspectives (e.g. Freedman & Combs, 1996), the self of the therapist (e.g. Flaskas & Perlesz, 1996) and reflecting processes (e.g. Andersen, 1987). Systemic supervision—with an emphasis on attempting to find a fit with developments in systemic therapy—has also had to consider how, for example, one develops a constructive, collaborative supervisory relationship within hierarchical structures without falling into the trap of seeing hierarchies (and power for that matter) as being somehow considered as intrinsically bad. Put differently, how do we make our supervision contact-centred?

This book addresses the contexts (whether they be gendered, cultural, clinical, theoretical, or ethical) in which supervision resides. Our aim is to take the richness that was evident in the 1999 conference and develop it for a wider audience.

The book is organized into four parts. The first part, "Setting the Context for Supervision", is based on plenary presentations at the original conference. These chapters define the terms of supervision by, for example, exploring differences between supervision and training; they introduce ways of formulating the relationship between supervisor and supervisee, and they place supervision in the wider contexts of ethics, gender, and culture.

The second part, "Perspectives on Training", clearly places supervision within the relationship between trainers and trainees. The larger questions—such as "is the supervision doing what it is intended to do?"—therefore come into prominence. These chapters present rationales for aspects of training and support these with feedback from trainees who have been on the receiving end.

The third part, "Perspectives on Practice", is clearly focused on practice with different client groups. Eating disorders, child protection, and work with refugees are the topics in which supervision is applied to help workers become "unstuck" in their work with client families.

Finally, since many in the field are thinking about clinical audit and evaluation of their work, the fourth part, "A Perspective on Evaluation", demonstrates one way in which supervision can be evaluated and can contribute to the process of clinical governance in public-sector agencies.

One of the challenges of putting together a multi-author book is to ensure that the reader does not become overwhelmed by a cacophony of different voices. Certainly these different perspectives will stimulate many thoughts, but we, as editors, also want to ease the reader's passage through the book and have therefore added our own comments sections to connect the parts and keep central systemic concepts in clear focus.

The common thread running through the book is the application of systemic thinking to the field of supervision. Each author has chosen his or her systemic concepts and defined them and applied them in his or her own way; however, the reader is reminded repeatedly about the importance of placing work in context; the necessity of gathering feedback to understand the supervision process; the tendency to see supervision as a multi-sided, relational process; the use of reflective spaces and dialogues to advance learning; the emphasis upon self-reflexivity or pausing to take stock of one's personal experience as a member of a wider interacting system; the understanding of how a "hierarchical" supervisory relationship can also be collaborative; and the placing of supervision in the context of the agency's need to evaluate.

David Campbell
Barry Mason

PART I

SETTING THE CONTEXT FOR SUPERVISION

CHAPTER ONE

Different levels of analysis in the supervisory process

Laura Fruggeri

I see supervision as a generative and transformative process—that is, as a process through which people develop abilities and skills. Before I present my ideas on supervision, however, some distinctions need to be made. The first section therefore outlines some theoretical specifications based upon which, in the later sections, I reflect on the different models of supervision.

THEORETICAL FRAMEWORK

Constructivism and constructionism: a both/and vs. an either/or perspective

Over the past decade, the systemic approach to psychotherapy has been much influenced by the constructivist and constructionist perspectives.

- *Constructivist perspective.* From this point of view, people make sense of their own experiences and act in relation to others according to a set of premises and beliefs. To put it more precisely, the actions and responses of people to the behaviours of others are a function of: (1) their individual systems of representations; (2) the meanings they attribute to behaviours and events according to their representational system(s); and (3) the type of responses that they intend to have from others. This set of premises and beliefs, or system of representations, comes from: (a) the specific position that people have in the interactive situation, (b) the experiences lived prior to the given interaction, and (c) the experiences that people are presently having within multiple relationships in several different social contexts.

In other words, people make sense of their world through a set of premises and beliefs, and this representational system is generated through interactive processes. It should be noted, though, that the constructivist perspective stresses overall the processes through which people construct their worlds and not the interactive processes through which beliefs are generated. The works of Von Foerster (1981), von Glasersfeld (1984), and Maturana and Varela (1980) have contributed to directing the attention of systemic therapists to the role that cognitive processes have in constructing reality.

- *Constructionist perspective.* Constructionists criticize the constructivist perspective as being too much centred upon the individual. The works of Gergen (1988), Harré (1989), and Shotter (1990) have all contributed to shifting the attention of systemic therapists away from cognition and towards language as the main process through which social worlds are generated. According to these authors, the emphasis on cognition hides the social nature of the process of constructing realities. Meanings, they claim, are not individually constructed. It is through communication and language that the participants of interactions negotiate the meanings of events and behaviours; they co-construct personal and social identities and co-define roles and relationships. In other words, they interactively generate and develop specific ways of organizing the world in which they live. Constructionism focuses on the social processes of constructing meanings.

The constructivist and the constructionist perspectives are usually considered as being oppositional, polarized stances within the field of systemic therapy. I, however, do not see these two perspectives as being in opposition; instead, I view them as being intertwined. Moreover, I see them as descriptions of different levels of the complexity of interactive processes.

The constructivism/constructionism polarization reflects, in my view, other polarizations such as cognition and communication (or language), individual and relationship, semantics and pragmatics, observed and observing systems, meanings and actions. But, as suggested by Varela (1979), these polarities can either be seen as distinctly separate and opposite entities or be considered as embricated entities. The term "embricated" implies that while the entities are different and irreducible one to the other, they nevertheless emerge one from the relationship with the other. Whether we see them as opposite or as embricated/connected entities depends on the perspective we take. If we take a both/and approach instead of an either/or approach, we can see that the polarities of the couple "constructivist and constructionist perspectives" are connected. In fact, from a both/and perspective, we can describe any interactive situation at a double level—at the level of individual construction and at the level of co-construction—and the two levels are intertwined.

When we choose to describe *the level of individual construction* involved in an interaction, we focus on how people take part in interactive processes. From this perspective it is possible to point out the ways in which people make sense of their world(s), including themselves, others, and the situations they cope with. It is also possible to point out how people act both according to the way they make sense of all this and in the pursuit of maintaining an equilibrium between all the different components of their own reality. So, when we describe the individual level of construction, we point out how people take part in interactions and we stress feelings, meanings, goals, and behaviours. We may also underline how behaviours are connected to feelings that are connected to meanings, which in turn are connected to behaviours that are connected to goals.

But while the participants in the interaction are engaged in these complex symbolic, behavioural, strategic, and self-validating processes, they also initiate a "dance"—which we can call coordination of behaviours, joint action, language game—through which they negotiate and co-construct meanings, identities, relationships, roles, and social realities. When we choose to describe this joint process, we point out the *level of co-construction.* From this perspective, we do not underline how people take part in an interaction; rather, we focus on what they do together.

The *level of co-construction* and the *level of individual construction* are linked through a recursive process. If we read the recursivity beginning from the level of co-construction, we can say that social interactions generate meanings and realities through which individuals define themselves and participate in interactive processes. But the same recursivity can be described starting from the individual level of construction: individuals are co-authors of a co-ordination of actions and meanings which gives shape to a social interaction through which individuals process are generated (Bateson & Bateson, 1987; Maturana & Varela, 1980; Moscovici, 1989).

The level of individual construction is stressed by constructivism, and the level of co-construction is emphasized by constructionism. These two perspectives can be combined and result in a complex point of view that guides us in the analysis of the interconnection of individual and relational constructions involved in any interaction. When people start an interaction, they bring with them other interactive stories that have generated specific meanings and social realities. It is from these previously constructed social realities that people engage in new interactions and give shape to a dance through which they co-construct new meanings and new social realities. As Karl Tomm puts it, "'Outer' interpersonal conversations become 'inner' intrapersonal conversations (in the form of conscious awareness and thinking) which support further outer conversations that modify inner thought, and so on" (Tomm, et al., 1992, pp. 117–118). It should be noted, though, that social interactions do not always construct change. Through social interactions, people might re-construct or perpetuate meanings and realities.

Levels of descriptions of the therapeutic process

The distinction between the individual and the co-construction levels of interaction is helpful when distinguishing between different levels of analysis of any therapeutic situation (Fruggeri, 1998).

At one level (individual construction) we focus on the therapist: on his or her thoughts, intentions, decisions, and language. We could, of course, have talked of goals, descriptions, ideas, and theoretical models—or even of prejudices, values, ideology, and actions. At the individual construction level of analysis, we pay attention to how all these elements connect with each other in a pattern that could be defined as "the way the therapist participates in the interaction with the client". Most conversations among therapists take this level into consideration—that is, the level of reflexivity between theoretical framework, attribution of meaning (descriptions), and actions. It is according to a theoretical model that therapists describe the situation as they do, and it is according to what they describe and to their theoretical model (or to their philosophical stance) that they make decisions to do this or that in order to help the client. It does not matter whether the theoretical framework is informed by social constructionism (e.g. the therapist decides to take a "not-knowing position") or whether the theoretical framework is strategic (e.g. the therapist decides to give a paradoxical prescription). In both cases, the therapeutic actions (which should not be confused with the therapeutic effects) emerge from an individual construction.

Of course, therapists are not the only ones who individually construct and act in the situation. Clients are engaged in the same kind of process. Therapists who have collected descriptions of how their clients viewed therapies have found interesting points for reflection. Here is an example:

> We had great expectations from that psychotherapy, and at the beginning things seemed to go very well: we all liked the doctor. He started by saying that first of all we had to picture the situation. But then, that picture was never ending. . . . He used to make us talk, talk, talk. . . . We were willing to do anything in order to change something. . . . We never talked about Luciano's problems . . . mainly of the past. . . . But Luciano was getting worse and worse. We expected the doctor

> to give us advice on what to do. We asked him questions, but he used to tell us to turn those questions to each other. Instead of answering questions himself, he was asking us questions all the time. Every once in a while he tried to make us see the positiveness of our situation, and that there wasn't much to change. We started to feel . . . I don't want to say cheated, but we started to feel not helped. [Cingolani, 1995, p. 117]

Clients do not have formal theoretical models to refer to; they have naive or implicit theories according to which they also make sense of what is happening and then act. Clients do not respond to the therapist according to what the theoretical model of the therapist states; they respond according to the sense they make of what the therapist does—that is, according to their own way of constructing the situation and in order to achieve their own goals, whatever these may be.

The individual construction level of the therapeutic situation can be described as in Figures 1.1 and 1.2. Figure 1.1 describes a therapist (T) who, according to his or her theoretical model (TM), analyses, listens, explains, invites, makes interventions, and tries to understand the client (C). Figure 1.2 represents a client (C) who, according to his or her implicit or naive theories (IT), makes sense of the therapist and the therapeutic situation and responds to the therapist (T).

While therapist and client are engaged in their individual processes of construction, they also participate together in a cooperative dance, a joint action through which they negotiate and co-construct who they are, what they are doing together, and what the situation is that they are involved in (Pearce & Cronen, 1980).

If the level of individual construction is characterized by self-validation, organizational closure, and recursivity, the level of co-construction is characterized by deuterolearning (Bateson, 1972),

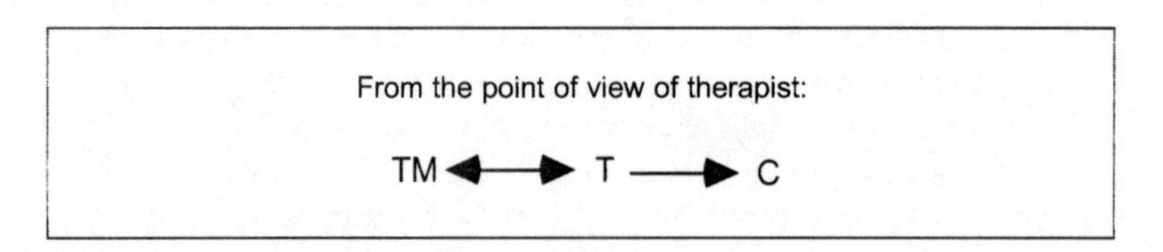

FIGURE 1.1

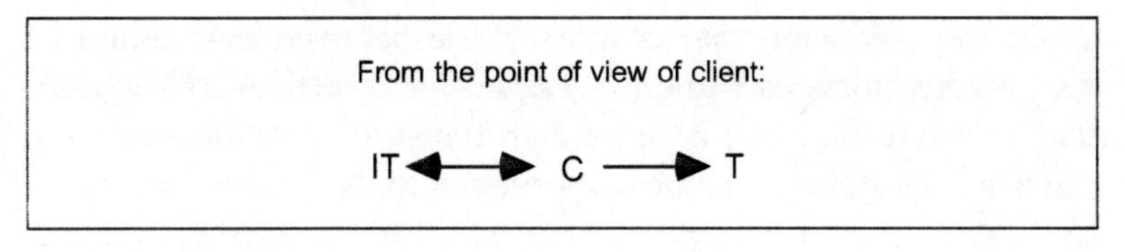

FIGURE 1.2

structural coupling (Maturana & Varela, 1980), and unintended consequences (Lannamann, 1991; Shotter, 1990).

We could say that any action of the therapist and the client can be reflexively connected to their representations, intentions, and goals, but the outcome (the effect of their actions) is generated through the constructive process in which therapist and client are co-authors, each one starting from his or her own premises and stories.

The co-construction level of the therapeutic situation can thus be described as in Figure 1.3. The focus in Figure 1.3 is on the double arrow that indicates the joint action of therapist and client. The analysis of this level of the therapeutic process does not pertain to the therapists' ideas or actions, goals or expectations, nor to the clients' ideas, actions, goals, or expectations. At this level, the analysis implies a description of interactions—that is, of the joint action of therapist and client and of the meanings generated through it.

I consider the distinction between the levels of individual construction and of co-construction to be central, as will be seen particularly when we come to talk about supervision. I also address later on the question of whether supervision deals with the level of individual construction or with that of co-construction. I want to underline here that in order to maintain the distinction between these two levels of interactive processes, it is necessary to

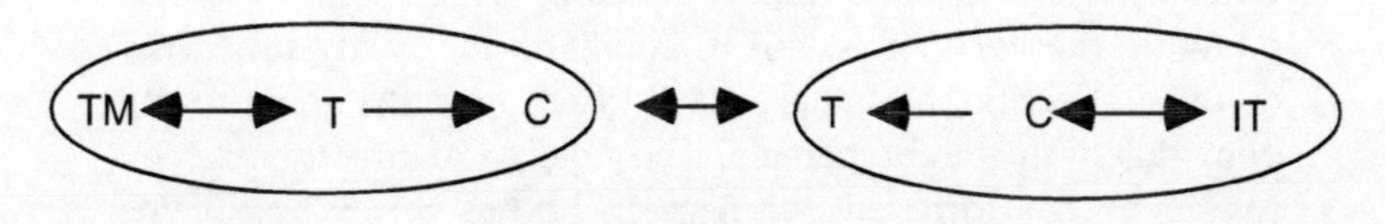

FIGURE 1.3

avoid the confusion that is often made between description of interactions and description of sequences of actions. As we say that a system (totality) is more than the sum of its elements, we can also say that interaction is more than the sequences of actions that compose it. A description such as: "The therapist spoke, and the client responded, and then the therapist responded, and the client spoke", is a description of the interactive process in terms of sequences of actions. If we want to describe it in terms of interaction, we should be able to say what they do together. In fact, while one speaks and the other responds, they might construct together pathology, or dependence, or change, or blame on someone, and so on.

Interdependence versus circularity

I shall introduce the last point I want to address in this section with John Percival's narrative of the treatment experienced by a gentleman in 1840:

> I would not always overcome my exasperation. But even then I was frequently influenced by a spirit of bravado and defiance of the doctors, to whom I knew my letters were subjected for inspection; I was determined, if they declared that my anger at being confined, and at my treatment, was a proof of my madness, that they should have evidence enough of it. . . . Even a deeper motive lay hid under all this violence of expression; and this may perhaps by many be deemed an insane motive: I knew that, of all the torments to which the mind is subject, there is none so shocking, so horrid to be endured as that of remorse for having injured or neglected those who deserved our esteem and consideration. I felt for my sisters, my brothers, and my mother: I knew they could not endure to look upon what they had done towards me, to whom they were once so attached, if they rightly understood it; that they could know no relief from the agony of that repentance which comes too late, gnawing the very vitals, but in believing me partly unworthy of their affection; and therefore I often gave the reins to my pen, that they might hereafter be able to justify themselves, saying he has forfeited our respect, he has thrown aside the regard due to his parentage and to his kindred—he has de-

served our contempt, and merited our abandonment of him. [reported in Bateson, 1978, p. 49]

When therapists talk about therapeutic processes, they often confine their conversations to a narrow context—that of the therapist–client interaction (the client being either a person or a family). All that is outside the therapy-room seems to disappear, as if clients changed or stayed the same only for what happens in the context of their relationship with therapists. But as John Percival explains to us, the way clients respond to therapists is connected with the meanings generated in the therapeutic setting with respect to other contexts of relationship. Conversely, whatever is going on in these relationships affects the process of therapy. The interpersonal process taking place in a therapeutic situation is then part of a broader network of interdependent relationships. This implies that the level of co-construction has more than just two co-authors. Describing the therapeutic process from this point of view means acknowledging the broader system of interdependent significant relationships (see Figure 1.4).

The analysis suggested by the diagram in Figure 1.4 is a description of the joint action of therapist and client, and of the meanings generated through it. But it is also a description of the effects that the joint action emerging in a context of interaction—for example, between therapist (T) and client (C)—has on all the other contexts of interactions involved in the situation—namely,

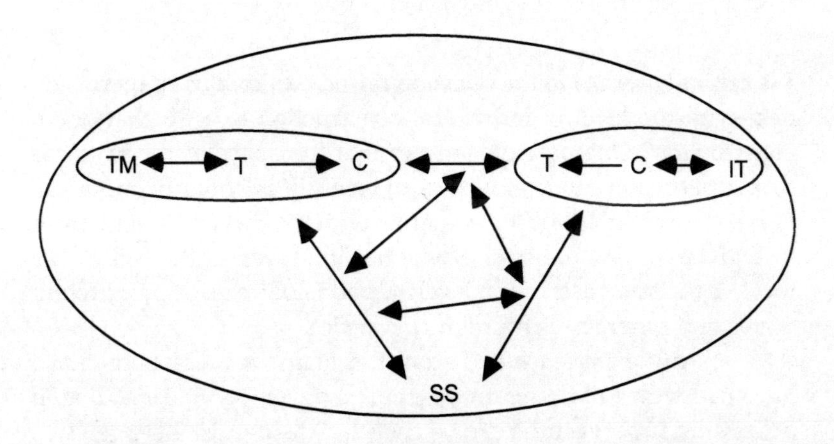

FIGURE 1.4

the relationship between the client and his or her significant systems (SS), and the relationship between the therapist and the client's significant system.

The idea of interdependence is different from that of circularity. The latter refers to relations of behaviours, the former to relations of relationships. The difference between interdependence and circularity is of the same kind as the difference between interaction and sequences of actions. In fact, circularity is a form of sequences of actions, while interdependence is a form of systems of interactions. The notion of circularity invites therapists to raise questions such as how the client responds to the therapist's questions, or how the client's significant others respond to the client's responses to the therapist. The notion of interdependence instead invites therapists to raise questions such as how what the therapist and client do together affects the relationship of the client to his or her significant others, or how what the client and his or her significant others do together affects the relationship of client and therapist. In other words, circularity raises questions at the level of individual construction; interdependence invites therapists to raise questions at the level of co-construction.

TWO MODELS OF SUPERVISION: "SUPERVISION AS TEACHING" AND "SUPERVISION AS REFLECTION ON ONE'S PRACTICE"

We can now return to the question raised earlier: does supervision deal with the level of individual construction or with that of co-construction? One possible answer that I propose to the reader is that supervision can deal with both levels. It is, though, important to be quite clear about the actual level that supervision addresses in a given situation, because whether it addresses the individual level or the co-construction level, supervision focuses on different issues and emerges as a different practice.

From my experience and from the many conversations that I have had with colleagues on this topic, I developed the idea that in discussing supervision it can be useful to distinguish between two models of supervision: "supervision as a practice of teaching a specific psychotherapeutic approach", and "supervision as a practice of reflection on someone's therapeutic practice".

These two different models of supervision are organized around two different foci of observation, description, or analysis. The first model deals with the level of individual construction implied in the therapeutic process, the second with the level of co-construction.

"*Supervision as a practice of teaching a specific psychotherapeutic approach*" is supervision that is centred on the supervisee and on his or her process of learning. Following the distinctions I made in the first section, my argument is that when the supervisory practice focuses on how supervisees develop a narrative, generate ideas, and behave with clients, reflect on their behaviours, explore their beliefs about families, and use their prejudices or biases, then supervision is addressing the individual level of construction—that is, the way the supervisees participate in the interaction with clients. It should be clear that talking about the ways one participates in an interaction does not mean that one is talking about social construction; it is only a pointer to the way an individual (a therapist, a supervisee) constructs the situation he or she is dealing with.

The methods through which "supervision as a practice of teaching" can be conducted may be different. Some authors identify the fit in the relationship between supervisor and supervisee as one of the most important aspects of a supervisory process (Scaife, 1993; Wilson, 1993), others view the supervisory process as a collaborative and egalitarian effort in which new meanings and change evolve through dialogue (Anderson & Swim, 1993), yet others suggest that the reflecting-team approach may enhance supervisees' skills and abilities (Reed, 1993). But what I want to underline here is that the focus of supervision in these cases is always the supervisees and the ways they approach their clients.

Supervision as a practice of teaching a specific psychotherapeutic approach can be represented as in Figure 1.5. This figure illustrates a supervisor–supervisee relationship that focuses on how the supervisee, in his or her position of therapist (T), applies or knows or generates ideas from a theoretical model in order to

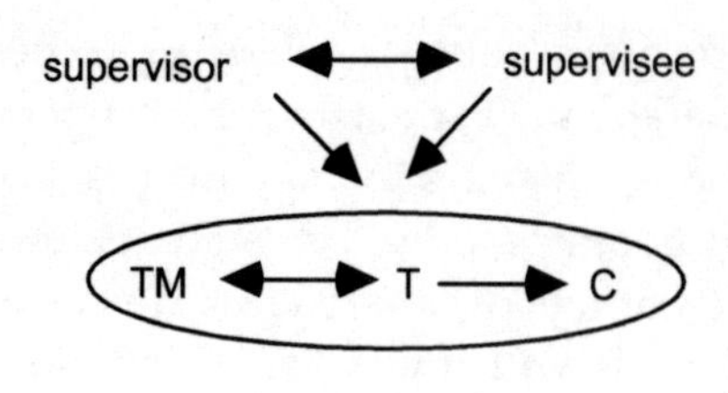

FIGURE 1.5

be helpful to a client (C)—that is, in trying to make sense of a client's situation, or in trying to act in the most useful way for the client to find relief from his or her situation.

In this context, questions that can be raised by supervisors are: "Why did you ask that question?" "How would you feel about introducing this idea?" "Don't you think there is a gender issue here?" "How would it be helpful to raise it?" "Why don't you try to suggest . . .?" "What is your hypothesis about . . .?" "It looks like certain words are central in this conversation—what about speaking more of . . .?" "What makes you think that? Is there any other way to describe this?"

The conversation taking place between supervisor and supervisee in the context of supervision as a practice of teaching, no matter how it is conducted, focuses on what the therapist/supervisee could do, or how the therapist/supervisee thinks or sees or feels or behaves.

"Supervision as a practice of reflection on someone's therapeutic practice" is supervision that is centred on the interaction of supervisee and client. The focus in this case is on what therapist/supervisee and client do together. Following again the distinctions I made in the first section, my argument is that when the supervisory process focuses on the therapist–client interaction, then it is addressing the co-construction level, since it stresses how the individual constructions of therapist and client coordinate to generate a social reality.

"Supervision as a practice of reflection" does not deal with ideas, attitudes, philosophical or ideological stances, behaviours, feelings, or emotions; rather, it deals with patterns and processes of interactions.

Supervision as a practice of reflection on someone's therapeutic practice can be represented as in Figure 1.6. As the figure shows, in this case the supervisor–supervisee relationship focuses on the interaction between the therapist (supervisee) and the client and the interdependent system of interactions of which they are part. We can imagine, then, a supervisor who, no matter what his or her model is, facilitates a supervisee to reflect on what people do together and on how this affects all the relationships involved.

Just as there are many different ways of teaching someone how to implement a therapeutic approach, there may also be many different ways to help people to reflect on the interdependent system of interaction. Personally, I follow a procedure that follows a line of questioning aimed at moving from descriptions of actions to description of interactions, from dyadic descriptions to triadic descriptions. This procedure is organized in four steps:

1. *Describe the case.* The supervisee is invited to tell the story of the therapy. Some supervisees include themselves in the story—that is, they also talk about what they did, felt, or thought in the situation—others do not include themselves and so the story told is all about clients. This is the first important

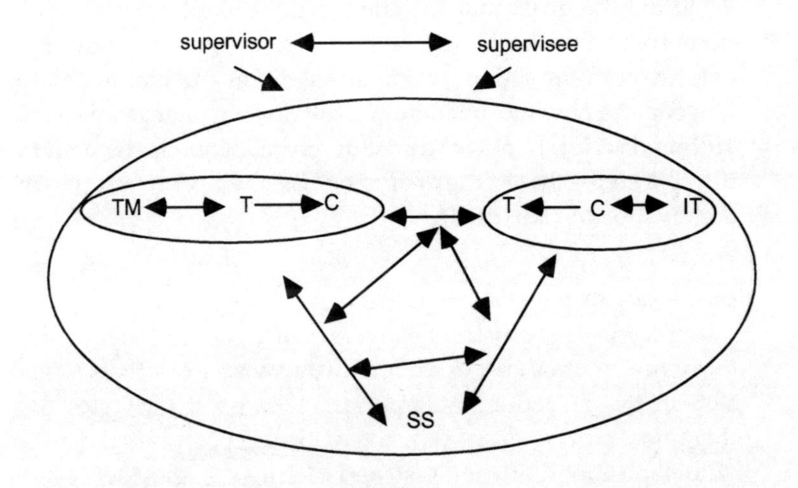

FIGURE 1.6

distinction that I want to underline, because the aim of supervision is that of moving from stories about clients to stories about the relationship between clients and therapists. So, in cases where supervisees tell a story centred on the client, the supervisor can facilitate supervisees to include themselves in the description as the first step that leads to a relational story. And this can simply be done by asking questions about therapists' behaviours, such as "And what did you do at that point?" or "And how did you respond to that?"

2. *Write down the characters who are involved in the case* (clients and their significant systems, including the therapist/supervisee and eventual professionals from different agencies). This step is not just descriptive of the people scenario. At this point, the supervisor asks questions that orient supervisees to reflect upon how all characters involved may understand the situation, what their possible goals are, and how they feel in relation to one another. During this phase, the supervisor helps the supervisees to decentralize from themselves and move from a self-reflexive position (What am I doing? What could I do? How could I change?) to a reflection on the points of view of the clients and all the others involved (How does the client see the therapist? What does the client think we are doing together? What are the goals that the client would like to reach?). The decentralization facilitates supervisees to recognize how clients are active in a therapeutic intervention and consequently to recognize how the outcome of a therapy is a joint action, a co-authored script. In other words, decentralization is the path to the next step—that is, the analysis of the therapeutic process at the level of co-construction.

3. *Describe the relationships that each one of them—therapist and client—has to the other in terms of what they do together.* For example: do they construct blame on someone, or dependence, or exclusion of others, or autonomy, or space for others? This step in the procedure is important because it facilitates the therapist/supervisee to draw the distinction between the individual positions of therapist and client (e.g. the therapist's intentions and the client's response) on the one hand, and the outcome of the interaction on the other. A therapist might have

the intention of opening space for the client to express him/herself and, in turn, the client might show a higher degree of confidence in developing his or her own narrative. And all this might also be a great relief for the client, but, at the same time, it could also develop a relationship of dependence in which the client becomes reliant on the therapist to express him/herself. Whether this is the case can only be known by reflecting upon the development of the relationship, not upon the actions and responses in a given situation and at a given moment.

4. *Reflect on how any change in any of the interactional contexts described would affect other contexts that compose the interdependent system of interactions*. For example, what happens in a client–parent relationship if the client shows higher levels of personal autonomy in his or her relationship with the therapist?

Following these steps, it is possible to produce what I call a "chart of interactions involved", which offers the supervisee a perspective from which he or she can position him/herself within the process of co-construction—that is, the process in which actions (including the therapist's actions) have meanings not according to theoretical models, but according to the dance performed together by all involved. It is from this perspective that the supervisee might start to develop ideas on how she or he should change in the relationship with the client.

DIFFERENT PRACTICES AND DIFFERENT CONTEXTS OF SUPERVISION

The difference that I see between "supervision as a practice of teaching a specific psychotherapeutic approach" and "supervision as a practice of reflection on someone's therapeutic practice" is that, in the first case, supervisor and supervisee focus on a model of psychotherapy and on how the supervisee implements it, whereas in the second, supervisor and supervisee focus on what people involved in the case do together and on how the supervisee positions him/herself in the interdependent system of interactions.

The distinction that I make here does not imply a judgement or an evaluation of the two models—that is, of whether or not one is better or worse than the other. It is a distinction between practices: one or the other can emerge as the more useful depending on the context.

In the case of a training course aimed at building the competences of trainees in a specific psychotherapeutic approach, "supervision as a practice of teaching" appears proper and consonant with the way the context is defined. That is:

1. The supervisee is a student and the supervisor is a teacher: this implies that the former, who is defined as the "one who is not-yet-knowing", asks to learn a therapeutic model; the latter, who is defined as the "one who knows" the model, agrees to teach it. I want to underline once again that it does not matter whether the therapeutic model implies directive or collaborative methods, objectivistic or constructionist perspectives. Trainees refer to an institute because they recognize the abilities of the trainers to teach them a method, a model, a perspective, or even how to develop a "not-knowing position".
2. The agreement that defines the relationship between trainees and trainer is centred on the model, with all its techniques, theoretical foundations, language expressions, and epistemological, moral, and ideological perspectives.
3. The ethics of acts, behaviours, and interventions of students and teachers reside, on the one hand, in the right of the student to be taught and to learn a model (this right includes that of being evaluated, i.e. to have feedback on how the learning is proceeding) and, on the other, in the responsibility of the teacher to allow this to occur (this responsibility includes that of evaluating the student's learning).

In this context, the supervisory process may—but we could say it should—address the individual level of construction. In the context of training, supervision usually focuses on how the trainee/therapist/supervisee participates in the interaction with client—that is, it focuses on how the student implements the theoretical model that he or she is learning. "Supervision as a practice of teaching" appears consonant with a training context. Of course, in a context of training, it may be proper also to orient the attention of students to the level of co-construction.

But there are circumstances when "supervision as a practice of teaching" does not appear proper. This is the case when a professional is invited to supervise other professionals who are already trained in a therapeutic model. The request made by supervisees to a supervisor is that of being helped in reflecting upon their own practice, with the aim of improving the competence that they already have in their own model. In this case, the context of supervision is defined in a completely different way:

1. Both supervisee and supervisor are professionals, and this implies that both the former and the latter are defined by their competence in a specific therapeutic approach. The supervisee and the supervisor can be trained in the same model or in different ones.
2. Nevertheless, in both cases, the agreement that defines the relationship between supervisor and supervisee is not centred on the model but on reflection upon the supervisee's practice. In fact, in the case of a shared model, supervisees might feel very confident in their expertise and yet want to develop skills in reflecting upon the way they implement their expertise in different situations. Of course, it is even more so the case when the supervisees have been trained in a therapeutic model that is different from that of the supervisor.
3. The ethics of acts, behaviours and interventions of supervisees and supervisors resides, on the one hand, in the right of the supervisees to learn from reflecting upon their own practice and to be respected in their professional competence, and, on the other, in the responsibility of the supervisors to facilitate this without asking the supervisees to give up to their theoretical model.

In this case, focusing the supervisory process on the individual level of construction—that is, on how the supervisee implements the theoretical model—might set a judgemental context or produce a shift from a symmetrical definition of relationship between supervisor and supervisee to an asymmetrical one. The supervisor, in this case, is called in as a facilitator not as teacher, and the model that I name "supervision as a practice of reflection on one's own practice" could emerge as more generative.

FINAL REMARKS

When supervision addresses the individual level of construction, it is centred either on how the supervisee acts and thinks or on how he or she could act or think instead. When supervision addresses the level of co-construction, it tends to orient the supervisee to position him/herself in the interdependent system of interaction involved in the case. So, if in the circumstance of a training it is proper for the supervisor to orient the way supervisees think or act, in circumstances that are different from training (such as peer supervision, supervision of team members with different educational background, and supervision of professionals already trained or experienced), it could be more consonant for the supervisor to set a context in which supervisees themselves can generate new ways of thinking or acting. The model proposed here of "supervision as a practice of reflection on one's practice" can represent a useful way to set such a generative context.

CHAPTER 2

Cultural issues in supervision

John Burnham & Queenie Harris

AN INTRODUCTION TO THE AUTHORS

We have created an introduction to ourselves around some useful questions about us posed by the editors.

How do we connect to systemic ideas?

As we participate in the development of the systemic culture, our current position is to say that we have relationships with many different ideas. At different times and for different reasons we have had a strong relationship with a particular idea, whereas at other times the relationship is more distant. We tend not to "abandon" old ideas but, rather, introduce new ideas, concepts and practices into our "ecology of ideas" (Bateson, 1972). Instead, therefore, of new ideas erasing old ideas, we think how the new ideas, as well as being useful in themselves, also help us to "recycle" existing ideas so that they are refreshed and can still be useful to us. Otherwise, we think that we would create theoretical ageism and promote a culture of obsolescence wherein only the new is privileged. Indeed, all cultures create relationships between tradition and newness. For example, the process of hypothesizing, though abandoned or discouraged by some, can be refreshed when a distinction is made between making a hypothesis (a particular idea) and hypothesizing (the ability to construct, deconstruct, and reconstruct ideas). The process of hypothesizing can be seen as part of the process of being transparent about the ideas and cultural values that are guiding a practitioner so that they become more available for scrutiny and change.

What are the working context(s) in which our work is done?

Our work together has been done within the context of Parkview Clinic (now part of Birmingham Children's Hospital Trust). Our supervisory practice includes practitioners who are circulating through the clinic as part of their training in nursing, psychiatry, social work, and psychology. It also includes a University of Birmingham validated course in systemic therapy, to which professionals come to train specifically as systemic therapists. Queenie also works at the Woodbourne Priory Hospital. John also works at the Kensington Consultation Centre (KCC) in London, where he supervises and is director of the Diploma in Systemic Teaching, Training and Supervision (DSTTS), which is a course validated by the University of Northumbria at Newcastle (UNN). These different contexts mean that we are working with people from different ethnic cultures and professional cultures.

Our personal contexts

While we have created and shared a professional context over a period of 23 years, our personal/professional contexts are somewhat different; we have dramatized the differences below in a replication of the opening to our plenary presentation at the conference that gave rise to this book.

PLAYING WITH CULTURE

A play of many meanings but with only one scene! (A systemic play in which each scene could be the last, including the first!)

Scene 1. Two professionals discussing their relative positions in the context of different aspects of culture.

QH (Asian-looking woman, standing and speaking in authoritative voice): "I am Dr. Harris. I am a Consultant Child & Adolescent Psychiatrist of 24 years' standing. I am a Fellow of the Royal College of Psychiatrists and have a Diploma in Psychological Medicine. I have Grandparent status in the field of Family Therapy and have also achieved this position naturally! I speak from within the dominant and superior medical discourse of expert opinion!" (Turning to JB she asks, imperiously "And just who are you?"

JB (white Caucasian man, sitting and speaking in hesitant, humble, tones): "I . . . I trained originally as a Social Worker and then re-trained as a family therapist. I speak from a minority position in the health service, but don't get me wrong. I am very grateful that the medical profession let me work alongside them . . . that's who I am."

QH (joining JB, sitting and speaking in a more gentle, empathic voice): "Well, I can connect with that as an Indian woman in the general culture and, in particular, within the medical discourse. I have experienced being marginalized and having to work really hard to progress in my career both as an Indian woman and a female doctor . . ."

JB (interrupting, stands up and speaks with authoritative voice while QH remains seated): "Well now, since we are on the topic of gender, I can speak with an authoritative male voice and take the lead in this discussion . . .

QH (interrupting, rises from her seat while JB sits down): "Hmmmmm . . . Yes, you are speaking with a dominant male voice, but you do seem to have what I hear as a regional and very probably working-class accent, whereas I speak securely from my upper-middle-class position. My father was an Engineer and I am married to a General Medical Practitioner and have children who are in the medical profession and married in the medical profession."

JB: "Oh, all right then . . . I suppose being a Newcastle United Football Club supporter doesn't count for much then, does it?"

Reflections on our personal/professional differences

In order to bring to life some of the varied cultural influences and power relations that have a bearing on practice and supervision, we chose to enact the above scene as this illustrates some of the many differences between us, playfully emphasizing them in their extremes, in a scripted way. They have been significant both in conflict and in coordination over the past 20 years. When we considered more deeply the issue of culture, we realized that there were multiple ways to think about culture: ethnic, professional, gender, class, and so on. We realize that we needed to consider these many "cultures" that gave meaning to the interactions between us and therefore influenced the supervision systems we create.

SYSTEMIC SUPERVISION

In the domain of systemic psychotherapy, an acceptance of the need for supervision has long been in place, though it has and is being effected in different ways in different models of practice and in different disciplines. The demand for greater accountability for one's practice, standards of practice, and registration processes has brought into sharp focus the need for more formalized structures that reflect this. The complex and challenging demands on practice inherent in living in a multicultural society has made more urgent the need to pay attention to the cultural context that might give meaning to behaviours. This is relevant both in therapy and in supervision. Inga-Britt Krause (1998) writes about therapy across cultures and defines culture as "a social construction created, maintained, reconstituted and changed through social relationships both public and private, general and intimate" (p. 4). This emerging concern with the influence of culture is evident in writing related to systemic practice (Stratton, 1998), systemic supervision (Down, 2000), and adult education (Brookfield, 1995). The Association for Family Therapy (AFT) and the Confederation of Family Therapy Training Institutions (CON-

FETTI) have produced two major contributions to this area through the magazine *Context* (Association for Family Therapy, 1995; CONFETTI, 1999).

The processes of therapy and supervision in any model or form are influenced by many different beliefs and experiences, and these determine the practices and outcomes of both supervision and therapy. As a practical way of reminding ourselves (therapists and supervisors) of this, we use the acronym SOCIAL GRRAACCES (gender, race, religion, age, ability, class, culture, ethnicity and sexuality) (Burnham, 1993; Roper-Hall, 1997). This prompt is useful in reminding us of the many strands that create a culture and that each one is important and may become foreground or background at different times. As we foreground one particular aspect and others become background, then the constructions we make may change. If we view these aspects as a "list", then they have one kind of usefulness. If we view these aspects as having a reflexive relationship with one another, then we are more likely to be alive to the complexity of culture. Consideration of the influence of culture includes race and ethnicity and is broadened to include our professional culture and "ethnicity" (Cutteridge, 1992). It can be usefully considered to include professional discipline, status, and specialist training. Each aspect will be influential to a greater or lesser extent at any one time, and the particular way in which the aspects are woven together will create a particular context.

The complex demands on practice inherent in living in a multicultural society make the dimension of cultural aspects in supervision an extremely important and challenging one. A particular event, behaviour, or communication may have quite different meanings and consequences in different cultures, and therefore what is an appropriate response in one culture may not be appropriate in another. Taking the position in therapy and supervision that "Only if culture becomes a problem or it emerges spontaneously will we deal with it" is, in our view, unsatisfactory. Such a position may be maintained by uncertainty about how to talk about culture. We have expressed the view elsewhere (Burnham & Harris, 1996) that if practitioners are willing to be "clumsy rather than clever", this makes the initial steps towards "cultural competence" easier to make.

It is important that systemic supervision uses its theoretical frames to facilitate the development of "cultural competence" (McGoldrick, 1994). This requires going beyond the dominant values and exploring the complexity of culture and cultural identity—not without values and judgements about what is adaptive, healthy, or normal, but without accepting unquestioningly the societal definitions of these culturally determined values. For example, it might be universally accepted that children need an adequate amount of sleep for their health and well-being. How this is achieved varies from culture to culture. Let us imagine a white Western family recently arrived in Bombay consulting an Indian family therapist in training. The mother complains that her 4-year-old child will not go to sleep by 6 p.m. and keeps getting into the parents' bed. The supervisory conversations would need to resist the temptation to see this complaint as "trivial" when considered in the light of the prevailing cultural norms about this issue. These norms would not necessarily see the child's behaviour as problematic and may, instead, see the parents' insistence on getting the child to sleep by a particular time and in a particular place as an ineffective way to achieve the goal of helping the child to get enough sleep. The therapist and supervisor would need to "step outside" their own cultural norms through adopting a posture of curiosity. From this position, they could explore the meaning of this issue both in the family's culture and in their own. Such an exploration may lead to both ways being seen as cultural constructions and so avoid pathologizing the white Western way of approaching children's need for sleep (however strange it may seem from within an Indian culture).

SOME USEFUL CONTEXTUAL DISTINCTIONS

We have found it useful to think about creating different domains or multiple contexts (Cronen & Pearce, 1985) when trying to deconstruct our work. In doing so, we would propose that supervisory activities can be divided into three important contexts when thinking about culture within the supervision of therapy:

1. the broad culture of supervisory practice
2. culture within the supervisory relationship
3. culture within the therapy relationship.

When creating these three distinctions, we find it useful to think about these "contextual levels" as having a reflexive relationship. Each level could be positioned as more influential at a particular time, for different reasons. A specific episode of supervision could have an effect that supports and confirms the prevailing culture of supervision used in the training context or could trigger a significant change in the prevailing culture. For example, if in the prevailing culture of supervision the reflecting team is seen as the way of conveying the team's ideas, then appreciative feedback from families is likely to confirm the cultural idea. If families say that listening to multiple perspectives is unhelpful and ask to hear the therapist's reflections directly, then the supervisory culture may challenge the orthodoxy of reflecting teams to enable therapists to both use reflecting teams and offer their own reflections to the family. The kind of culture of supervision that exists in an agency will create certain resources and restraints for each supervisory relationship.

We now look in more detail at each of these three distinctions.

The broad culture of supervisory practice

By the culture of supervision we mean the training and educational context in which the supervisory relationships are constructed. This culture is constituted by professional associations, journals, and conferences as well as published codes of ethics and practice. More specifically, it is created by how a training agency describes its courses; how multicultural is the staff group; how the issue of culture is addressed from the beginning of creating a relationship between supervisors and supervisees and the practices of assessment; and how culture figures in the creation of learning agreements (Knowles, 1990) and the process of experiential learning (Kolb, 1984). From the outset, this context will be very influential in creating how particular supervisory relationships are enacted and therapy practised. For example, the application form for the systemic training course in Birmingham includes the request:

> "Ethnicity: In your own words and in your own ways, please describe your ethnic identity and cultural belonging."

This is one way of foregrounding the issue from the beginning, and many applicants have expressed appreciation for this opportunity to define themselves. It also requires everyone to draw from their own cultural narrative rather than just "ticking a box". Answering this question seems to create a spirit of self-reflexivity that can be continued and revisited on the course through such processes as the cultural genogram (Hardy & Laszloffy, 1995).

We have chosen to begin with this level since the culture of the training context in which supervisors and supervisees work together in creating therapy for clients will have a major contextual influence on how team culture develops and particular relationships are defined. Many models support a style of supervisory practice that is isomorphic with the theoretical ideas that influence the therapy it practices. We would propose that these are useful concepts but we also borrow from the field of education (Brookfield, 1995; Bruner, 1986; hooks, 1994; Knowles, 1990; Kolb, 1984). Bruner (1986) proposes that we treat education as a specialized institution within culture in which "a culture is as much a forum for negotiating and re-negotiating meaning and for explicating action as it is a set of rules or specifications for action" (p. 123).

Of particular significance from the world of education are the ideas from bell hooks, a black, radical intellectual and cultural critic. Many of the black supervisors in training at KCC have spoken how her book, *Teaching to Transgress: Education as the Practice of Freedom* (1994), which is required reading on the DSTTS course, has inspired them to develop their practice as educators and supervisors. In a chapter entitled "Embracing Change: Teaching a Multicultural World", hooks describes in greater detail how she sets about creating "engaged pedagogy". It is an intensely personal account of a politicizing process.

She and a colleague proceeded by holding closed meetings in which teaching staff could express their fears and uncertainties about the likely and unlikely effects of the changes involved in practising multicultural teaching. Meetings were then opened to international speakers, who discussed their experiences in making this paradigmatic shift. She persisted in democratizing her classes in the face of initial protests from students. As one student is quoted as saying: "We take your class. We learn to look at the world from a critical standpoint, one that considers race, sex and class. And we can't enjoy life anymore." This convinced hooks of the need for compassion towards those who are reinventing their worlds, and she spent more time in explaining the philosophy of the classes:

- entering the classroom with a belief that building community is necessary to create a climate of openness and intellectual rigour
- focusing on community rather than safety creates a sense of shared commitment and a common good that binds us all
- ideally we all share the common desire to learn, to actively receive knowledge and live more fully in the world

and from these philosophies develop practices such as:

- actively recognizing the value of each individual voice through such practices as students keeping journals and reading out loud to the rest of the class extracts from these journals (at least once, irrespective of class size)
- hearing one another is a sign of recognition and no one remains invisible.

Students are made aware that such practices are a condition of attending her class.

hooks shares her feeling that

> When I first entered the multicultural, multiethnic classroom setting I was unprepared. I did not know how to cope effectively with so much "difference". . . . This is the case with most educators. As I worked to create teaching strategies that would make a space for multicultural learning, I had to recognize and learn different "cultural codes". *This act alone transforms the classroom.* [p. 41, emphasis added]

She also learnt to accept that the sharing of ideas and information does not progress as quickly as it may in homogeneous settings.

Many supervisors who only supervise white people may question why they would need to consider these issues. hooks' response is that

> it is so crucial that "whiteness" be studied, understood, discussed—so that everyone learns that affirmation of multiculturalism, and an unbiased, inclusive perspective, can and should be present whether or not people of colour are present. [p. 43]

The importance of training culturally competent therapists has implications for the training of both therapists and supervisors in the abilities necessary to bring forth these abilities. Creating a multicultural culture of supervision requires that more black and ethnic-minority professionals are included in training, both as therapists and as supervisors. The following examples indicates some of the complex issues in these circumstances.

Therapist in training

> *Case example: "The native informant"*
>
> A supervisor met an articulate young British Indian trainee and quite quickly recognized her knowledge and experience as a potential resource to the training group on cultural matters. An invitation intended to be affirmative was extended to the trainee, but to the supervisors surprise and disappointment the supervisee politely declined. She explained that, indeed, she was well able to speak from this position and, indeed, often conducted successful workshops on this topic. However, she felt that she had to avoid taking this position as teacher as she felt she would not be able to fully use and benefit from the position of being a trainee.

Learning points: The student was drawing attention to her wish not to become what hooks (1994) has called the "native informant" (p. 44) and Radovanovic (1993) refers to as a "prisoner of identity". This episode is reminiscent of other situations in which, whenever a member of a training group is perceived as having, or declares him/herself as having, a particular cultural heritage or quality, a pattern can develop in which whenever such an issue arises then "all eyes turn" to that particular person as the expert in that particular domain. This may well accord the person some status in the group and make him or her feel valued. However, if the pattern becomes entrenched, then the person may feel "trapped" into that position and be unable to experiment with speaking and acting from other positions. In addition, the other members of the group come to rely on that person and do not do valuable work on developing their own voice in relation to that topic.

Within hooks' thinking, it is important not to stereotype, even positively, when developing a culture of supervision. This position may be seen to contradict the "affirmative-action" movement, but the preceding example gives a sense of how it can have disadvantages. The course run by Ann Miller at the Marlborough Family Service in London specifically to train family therapists who are from ethnic minorities backgrounds is breaking new ground in this area of training.

Supervisor in training

Case example: "Withholding, with-holding"

Morris Mohlala, a black South African training as a systemic supervisor, recounted an experience where he was supervising a group in which he was the only black person. During the post-session discussion, one of the therapists in training made a comment/statement that could have been regarded as racist or culturally insensitive. Morris initially felt the pull to respond in a linear fashion "I was the only black person present—this positions me in a way that prescribes certain actions." Morris said that if he had been a peer member of the group, he would have addressed/challenged the remark directly. Instead, Morris decided to use a position we had discussed during supervision training called "to withhold, with-holding". This position involves the supervisor withholding (not immediately voicing his or her own views) while "holding" (supporting the group members) during the potentially uncomfortable phase of exploring the effects of such statements. Adopting this supervisory posture, Morris decided to withhold his own views to create space for students' views and continued to participate with-holding (giving support) so that the students could make use of the space created. Morris participated with gentle persistence, asking questions within the group about the views expressed. This helped to generate a reflective discussion during which these views were deconstructed in ways that enhanced the self-reflexivity of both the students and the supervisor, in relation to this kind of comment. Morris summarized his learning thus: "My usual response would have been linear and positioned me at the level of the person [who expressed the comments] rather than at the level of the group. When I positioned myself at the level of the group by asking, this enhanced the group's ability to reposition and moved the learning position from singular and linear to interactive and circular."*

Learning points: This area of training/supervision, like others, evokes strong feelings related to power (Down 2000). It can be difficult in training contexts to decide how to respond when comments are made that can be regarded as inappropriate, insensitive, or racist. Supervisors are faced with difficult situations, wondering when to close down a particular form of speaking and "set forth" their own ideas or the declared position of the training syllabus, and when to withhold these thoughts and "bring forth" others' views, creating a context for becoming culturally competent through self-reflexivity. This kind of situation has been described by Schön (1987) as "knowing-in-action".

Different kinds of supervision create different cultures and different cultures create different forms of supervision. For example, supervision by report may create a monoculture in which the voice of the therapist is privileged over the client's since the client's voice is heard through the construction of the therapist. Live supervision may be more likely to create a cosmopolitan

---

*Our thanks to Morris Mohlala, of the Child Guidance Service, Plumstead Health Centre, for his work in creating this example.

culture (Pearce, 1989) in which all voices can be heard as they are spoken.

Culture within the supervision relationship

The second of our three distinctions is that of the influence of culture in the relationship between the supervisor and therapist. The way in which the supervisor–supervisee relationship is defined at any particular point in time will have a major influence on episodes of supervision. This section explores how culture can act as a significant contextual influence in the supervisory process.

Case example: "Good Trainee/Bad Trainee"

The supervisor, JB, was concerned with the development of a trainee in the group who was from a different culture from himself. A young Japanese woman appeared to be "mimicking" the trainer and not seeming to progress in expressing her own opinions and showing her learning. She regularly referred and deferred to the supervisor, thus privileging the trainer's voice. This was becoming a problem both in her relationships with clients (always asking the supervisor what to do) and in the training relationship (JB was beginning to think that the student was unable to show initiative and would not pass the course). He consulted QH. They explored this culturally and hypothesized around the areas of personal and professional life-scripts and how different cultural values and deontic operators may be influencing the training episodes. They constructed the "loop" diagram shown in Figure 2.1, to see if this might offer a different view of the problem. This loop was shared with the student, who looked relieved and said it bore a close connection to her experience. She was also beginning to feel frustrated that she was not able to speak out in the way she observed other members of the group doing. The loop was "broken" by exploring the affordances that were possible when acting from within the context of a professional script rather than a personal script. In the culture of the course, a

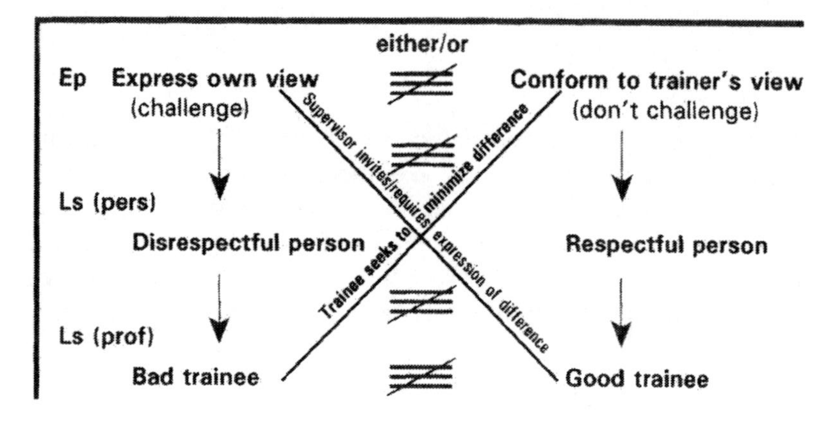

FIGURE 2.1 The loop diagram
(inspired by Cronen & Pearce, 1985)

professional script permitted and required students to express their own views. This new "freedom" enabled the trainee to act differently not only within the supervisory relationship but also within therapy relationships. These issues can be understood in the context of educational relationships rather than therapeutic relationships.

Learning points: Speaking generally, it is important to think about the relative expertise between the supervisor and supervisee and how potential resources do not become restraints. Take, for example, a situation where the therapist and family "share" the same culture but this culture is different from the supervisor's. This relational scenario could lead to a situation where the therapist is thinking, "This is a family from my culture therefore I should know what to do, be a better therapist, etc.", and therefore may feel restrained from using the supervisor as a resource. The supervisor might be thinking, "Well, I must respect the expertise of the supervisee with this family", and may therefore feel hesitant about making their expertise available to the work in progress. Similarly, the situation may be that the therapist is working with a family perceived as culturally different from him/herself but culturally similar to the supervisor. It could be easy for the therapist to think, "Well, I'd better rely on the supervisor's expertise here", and become preoccupied with what the supervisor may or may not be thinking. This could lead to an escalating complementarity where the more the therapist relies on the supervisor, the more the supervisor feels that she or he has to assist the therapist. During the "ritual of clinical supervision" (Burnham, 1993), it is important to create second-order hypotheses that explore the relationship between supervisor and supervisee. These issues can also be considered in other contexts where learning agreements (long- and short-term) are created and revised.

Teams and team work

The conceptual distinction between observed and observing systems becomes important when it helps a professional or team to recognize their descriptions as inscriptions and to see how their approach, methods, and techniques (Burnham, 1992) help to co-create what kind of families they meet, see, and work with.

What are the constraints and affordances in the use of reflecting teams in the promotion of cultural understandings? How can the practice of reflecting teams facilitate cultural understandings? Are there constraints in the use of this practice with certain cultural groups? For example, what consideration needs to be given to the linguistic abilities of family members from ethnic backgrounds, who may find intimidating or overwhelming the processes of reflecting teams, rooted as they are in a predominantly Western concept of therapy? What closer consideration needs to be given with regard to language, hierarchically organized traditional families, and the subjugated voices within them?

In this section, we have considered the influence of culture in the supervisory relationship which creates an important context for and is reflexively influenced by "what goes on in the room"—that is, the relationship between the therapist and family.

Culture within the therapy relationship

In this third and final distinction, that of culture within the therapy relationship, we are concerned with exploring how supervision enables the therapist to utilize systemic concepts in the exploration of cultural influences and meanings of a given problem and the process of therapy. Respect for the observed-system position can have advantages when an observer rigorously devotes time and effort to the apparently "selfless" study of a subject. Knowledge is constructed that acts as general guidelines for practitioners who are contemplating working with families whose ethnic group is different from their own. For example, knowledge of resources needed for work with these families would include learning about different cultures, the employment of interpreters rather than using family members as interpreters, and drawing on the experience of other families sharing the same cultural background. Knowledge and familiarity with the work of voluntary agencies involved with families from ethnic minorities with particular problems—for example, domestic violence or the care of the elderly—can help therapists enable particular families to connect with them (Burnham & Harris, 1996).

The development of culturally competent therapists requires supervisors to help therapists to question people from their own culture about culture. It seems obvious that a supervisor will be pleased to see a therapist developing cultural competence with clients who are from a different culture from that of the therapist (e.g. see Carter & McGoldrick, 1989; Hannah, 1994; Lau, 1986, 1988; McGoldrick, Pearce, & Giordano, 1982). Less obvious but equally important, it is important to develop those same abilities with clients from the same culture. Clients from the same/similar culture as the therapist may expect the therapist to "know" how things are for them culturally. We have introduced a position called the "as-if not-knowing position" to help therapists enter this potentially difficult area (Harris & Burnham, 1997).

Case example: "What you see is not all that you get"

JB was interviewing a couple. The wife was of Indian origin and the husband was white English. QH was the supervisor. She noticed that JB repeatedly tended to spend more time engaging the wife in conversation and more fully explored culturally based meanings for some of her ideas and attitudes, while seeming to ignore doing the same with the husband. This observation was offered, and the therapist was able to continue by exploring the husband's cultural concepts and practices. Post-session discussion raised the following issues. JB was following "good cultural competence practice" by actively exploring someone who was visibly different from himself and not assuming that the dominant white cultural discourse prevailed; however, simultaneously he was conforming to the dominant white cultural discourse by appearing to assume that he already knew what the person who looked similar to himself would think and do. The supervisor, QH, who is Indian, could have been pleased to see the white therapist attending to what was for him difference (for her sameness) but may have missed an opportunity to assist the therapist in exploring "whiteness".

Learning points: Culturally speaking, working with "sameness" is as important as working with "difference". Otherwise, white/majority therapists confirm the idea that it is ethnic minorities who have culture. Difference seems to be a foregrounded notion in systemic culture, and so we have to challenge—be curious about—our own systemic discourse. Within sameness, there are many differences; these kinds of differences are not so obvious and require the "discipline of curiosity" to emerge.

We regard an ability to adopt a posture of contextual curiosity as essential if therapeutic conversations are to be created. However, one needs to guard against the development of a myth that more knowledge necessarily means less racism, or that more knowledge necessarily means more understanding (Burnham & Harris, 1996).

Cultural reflexivity

How is the "cultural reflexivity" of a therapist to be promoted in a supervisory relationship? How does one participate in a process that maximizes the opportunity for therapists in training to experience freedom from constraining ideas derived from professional and personal beliefs influencing their practice and hope for the possibility of a different kind of culturally sensitive practice to emerge? One of the most useful questions we have found is for the supervisor to request that the therapist (and indeed the supervisor) ask him/herself the same kind of questions as he or she is asking the family. For example, if a therapist is enquiring about the particular aspects of a family's culture, this can lead to the therapist becoming fixed in a first-order system perspective, no matter how useful the questions are. If the therapist (and supervisor and other team members) also asks him/herself the same kinds of questions, it can help him or her become aware of his or her own cultural influences in relation to the same issues as are being talked about with the family. This awareness may then be used to avoid unhelpful relations and create a therapeutic direction in work with the family.

Case example: "Great expectations"

An Indian mother and her daughter were being seen by a white female therapist in training. The therapist moved on after five sessions (due to training rotation) and, at the end of her final session with the family, handed over to a member of staff who was Indian, female, and experienced. The therapist and white supervisory team were expecting (a complacent hypothesis) that there would be a strong cultural rapport between family and therapist, but, on the contrary, the mother, literally, "backed off", looking and sounding hesitant. This issue was raised and discussed at the beginning of the next session. The mother expressed her doubts as her concern that someone from their own culture would be likely to attempt to persuade them to return to the abusive husband that she had left. After discussion, she expressed some reassurance thus: "Now that I know that you are from the south of India, I feel better, since you are more likely to be flexible about these things."

Learning points: This example shows the usefulness of challenging common assumptions such as "Families are always better helped if seen by a therapist from the same background."

From the point of view of therapists, they may feel a greater expectation to be "expert" within their own culture and so act as if they should not need a supervisor. From the point of view of supervisors, they may feel intrusive by supervising in their "usual way" when both therapist and family are culturally the same as each other but different from the supervisor. In this situation, the supervisor may become less confident to supervise and risk depriving the therapist of his or her resources. From the supervisor's point of view, we have found it important to supervise from the position of systemic trainer working with process rather than cultural expert working with content. In this way, the supervisor can be respectful and continue to use his or her skills by asking such questions as: "Do you experience the family as viewing you more as an Asian woman or as a professional therapist? When you are sitting with a family, when do you find yourself speaking from the Indian culture and when do you find yourself speaking from the systemic culture?" In our experience, we find that this kind of approach achieves a both/and position that uses the expertise of therapist and supervisor in the co-construction of cultural competence.

In developing the culturally reflexive abilities of a therapist, it can be very helpful to use techniques such as "internalized-other interviewing" (IOI) developed by David Epston (1993) and Karl Tomm (workshop handouts/personal communications). This would involve interviewing a therapist or supervisor as if he or she were a current or past client/trainee. This process can help the therapist to become aware of his or her awareness and aware of aspects that he or she has made assumptions about but has not enquired about. This process can be with a client/trainee from the same or a different culture (see Burnham, 2000, for further details about the process of IOI).

GENERAL THEMES WE REGARD AS IMPORTANT

Some important themes have emerged in our work which we think facilitate conversations about culture in all aspects of supervision.

- *Creating a context that is safe and facilitative*

  Supervision both at peer and training levels is enhanced in a context that is regarded as safe and facilitative, in which different people from different cultural and professional backgrounds can reflect on their life's experiences and attitudes and their practice when encountering cultural differences. The process of hypothesizing is invaluable in promoting such conversations.

- *Understanding the family's/individual's interpretation of their own culture*

  There is a need to explore and understand every family's/individual's adaptation and interpretation of their own culture.

- *Emphasis on learning from shared experiences*

  The importance of sharing and learning from each other's experiences, rather than finding answers for difficult questions or defining particular models of practice from a position as experts, must be emphasized. This can free participants in a supervisory relationship from the idea that there is a definitive answer to each dilemma and can guide them towards constructing models of practice. This is particularly relevant to discussions in a supervision context.

- *Usefulness of ideas, rather than right or wrong ideas*

  Connections between ideas should be made, rather than deciding which is the right or wrong idea. All ideas discussed and considered need to be viewed in terms of how useful they are, rather than whether they are right or wrong. Such an attitude promotes an atmosphere of respect for each other and the ideas expressed.

An orientation such as this enables one to operate towards a position of "safe uncertainty" which as proposed by Barry Mason (1993) is to be regarded as an evolving state of being. Lang, Little, and Cronen (1990) propose that "The systemic position is that persons have the opportunity to participate in the elaboration, maintenance or change of diverse patterns of living through the ability to co-create a multiplicity of stories in action" (p. 1).

THE FUTURE?

We close with some questions that are intended to keep alive the spirit of rigorous curiosity that has enabled the systemic field to come this far in promoting cultural competence.

What needs to happen to enable more therapists from minority groups to participate more fully as supervisors and trainers? The work already being done in promoting the training of therapists from ethnic minority groups is a worthy beginning. However, when there is a greater representation of these groups at conferences such as the one on which this volume is based, and their work is celebrated in family therapy journals, then one might have the evidence of efforts made in this direction. As long as the contribution of British family therapists from ethnic-minority groups and the celebration of their work continues to be marginalized, the *status quo* in discourses around dominance and subjugation and other discourses is maintained. What encouragement does this offer those from minority groups in the training context to sustain their participation in rigorous training programmes?

Careful consideration in training programmes in this country also needs to be given to the training of students from within Eastern cultures. What responsibilities do supervisors have in preparing them for working in their own countries of origin, rather than equipping them with skills and ways of thinking that privilege the "Western" way of doing therapy? These are some of the issues that cultural aspects in supervision need also to address.

Roland Littlewood (1992) asks the question: "Is there a universal thing called therapy?" Can the same question be posed about supervision?

PART II

PERSPECTIVES ON TRAINING

CHAPTER 3

A reflective recording format for supervisors and trainees

Barry Mason

As systemic clinicians and supervisors we try to contribute to the creation of useful change. Our beliefs about change influence both our clinical and supervisory practice and the nature of clinical and supervisory relationships. One way that I see change is as follows:

> For change to happen we need to become less certain of the positions we hold. When we become less certain of the positions we hold we are more likely to become receptive to other possibilities, other meanings we might put to events. If we can become more open to the possible influences of other perspectives we open up space to be stated and heard. [Mason, 1994, p. 112]

Consistent with this definition of change are the therapeutic and supervisory stances that I take in relation to both clients and supervisees. This can be best described as working towards positions of safe uncertainty (Mason, 1993), safe uncertainty being a framework for establishing a safe-enough context to take risks, "orientating one away from certainty to fit" (p. 194) and authoritative doubt (Mason, 1993, 1999). The latter can be described as the ownership of expertise in the context of uncertainty, as opposed to either an absolutist position of knowing or a misplaced and disingenuous position of "not knowing" (Anderson & Goolishian, 1992b), particularly, if "not knowing" is misread as a disowning of expertise. In relation to my practice as a supervisor, it is important that all elements of supervisory practice are consistent with such principles.

In the early 1990s (at the same time as I was starting to develop some of the above ideas), I had started to address in more detail how the written recording process might be improved in the context of the (live) clinical supervision of experienced professionals in the Master's training programme in family and systemic psychotherapy at the Institute of Family Therapy in London. How could the recording process become more consistent with the ideas about change highlighted above? While clinical supervisors within the institute used a systemic approach in the way people were trained, in that we believed we were taking a position consistent with the interrelatedness of elements within a system, it seemed to me at this time that the written recording of the clinical process was, essentially, limited systemically.

This chapter seeks to promote an integrated approach to the written recording of clinical work and, in doing so, to contribute to a more systemic perspective. In particular, I would suggest that, among other things, such a format enables the supervisor to track in a creative and structured manner the development of the trainees' progress or lack of it. The format has now been used for over nine years in advanced programmes and more recently as part of portfolio developments in intermediate programmes.

THE RECORDING FORM

The recording form aims to help trainees (and the supervisor) develop a rigorous reflectiveness about practice. It is filled out for every clinical session. The form combines theory, technique, research, ethics, the therapeutic utilization of self, supervision, and peer consultation. The different headings making up the form are:

1. Client code—for example, "Mr and Mrs A" (for purposes of confidentiality).
2. Date of session.
3. Session number.
4. People present at the session.
5. Nature of referral (if first session).
6. Genogram.
7. Relevant research findings.
8. Working hypotheses.
9. Main themes to emerge:
   a. for clients
   b. for trainee
   c. for those behind the one-way screen (if used)
   d. for supervision.
10. End-of-session message (if given) or a summary of the reflecting team discussion.
11. Theoretical concepts used.
12. Techniques/skills used.
13. Issues pertaining to self.
14. Ethical issues.
15. Reflections on the writing-up of the interview.
16. Reflections of the trainee's consulting partner.

The majority of these headings are discussed below. Where relevant, brief extracts from the records of former trainees have been included as examples.

Genogram

The genogram has been a useful tool in family therapy for many years (Byng-Hall, 1995; Lieberman, 1979; McGoldrick & Gerson, 1985). More recently, race and culture have become a much more integral part of genogram thinking and practice. (Hardy &

Laszloffy, 1995). One of the most useful qualities of such a tool is that it helps therapists develop a map of relationships and thus contributes to the generation of ideas that may be useful in developing effective work. Whatever model of family therapy is being used, irrespective of whether it is in the context of a training programme, I believe it important that a sense of history is never marginalized. The genogram should therefore always be readily available, both to re-visit ideas and to add relevant information as it emerges from session to session. It is recommended that the genogram should be developed on a separate sheet of paper and placed at the front of the file for easy access. It is also important that the genogram include as an attachment any history of professional-network involvement with the family.

Relevant research findings

Sprenkle and Moon (1996) highlight the fact that the practice of family therapy, the research of family therapy, and research useful to family therapy have not necessarily been in harmony. It has seemed as if they have sometimes been disconnected worlds that have met reluctantly rather than from a perspective of being related and mutually influencing activities. Clinical interviewing, after all, can be said to be research endeavour. By having research as a core element of the recording process, a statement is made by the supervisor about the nature of interrelatedness between different elements of clinical development. Relevant research is defined here as not only about the results of qualitative or quantitative enquiry, but also published material that addresses issues relevant to the therapy (e.g, ideas about the treatment of eating disorders) but may not necessarily have research methodology as a primary element in the work. The research findings may or may not have a systemic basis. If they do not, this is by no means problematic for, as systemic thinkers and practitioners, we are surely interested in different ways of seeing. The important issue for the supervisor is to encourage the trainee to explore how the non-systemic research can be utilized systemically.

So, if a trainee has a referral of a reconstituted family, he or she will be expected to explore the relevant literature in that area and, in discussions within the supervision group, show how these findings are influencing his or her thinking and practice in working with the family.

Example

A trainee therapist was working with a white couple in their 60s who referred themselves to the institute because of long-standing disagreements in their relationship. After a few sessions the trainee noted her anxiety about how much responsibility she felt as the therapist in trying to sort out the difficulties presented. After the fourth session, she came upon a section on therapeutic responsibility in an article written by Cecchin (1987). Cecchin put forward the view that therapeutic responsibility begins with seeing one's own position in the system and that often this means sometimes recognizing what little power one may have. This led to the trainee starting to feel less of an overwhelming responsibility for "solving the couple's difficulties".

Working Hypotheses

Just as one cannot not communicate (Watzlawick, Beavin, & Jackson, 1967), so I would suggest that one cannot not hypothesize. There has, unfortunately, been a retreat from hypothesizing in the last few years, seemingly based on the idea that to hypothesize brings preconceived ideas into play, a "knowing" position into the work. Given that a "not knowing" position (Anderson & Goolishian, 1992b) has become a popular way of thinking in the last few years, one can see why for some people hypothesizing may be akin to being *persona non grata*. Interestingly, this development comes despite Anderson and Goolishian stating that their ideas are not about not having a position. Anderson (1997) seems to have realized later that the term "not knowing" has at times been taken too literally and in attempting to redress the balance quotes Jacques Derrida by noting that "not knowing" "does not mean that we know nothing" (p. 137). The "not-knowing" position could be said to belong to the category of concepts that don't exactly mean what they literally say (cf. neutrality, Selvini Palazzoli, Boscolo, Cecchin, & Prata, 1980). I therefore encourage trainees to explore moving from taking a position of "not knowing" to that of authoritative doubt (Mason, 1999), which I feel is a clearer expression of what actually happens in practice.

Hypothesizing does not mean, in my view, that one is forming opinions to which one is totally committed or is going to impose on clients. Rather, hypothesizing is to help one get into a frame of mind that allows openness to different ways of seeing. As a supervisor, therefore, I encourage supervisees not only to be curious (Cecchin, 1987) about what they might wish to explore with clients but to own their expertise, to take a position of authoritative doubt, and to take the risk of adopting a position about what may be happening in both the family and the therapeutic systems. Committing the position to the written word is also part of this process of owning what the trainee thinks.

Example

The W family were referred to the supervision group because of the concerns the couple had regarding the "acting-out" behaviour of their two sons, aged 11 and 12 years. The couple, a white British man and a woman originally from Eastern Europe, had been separated for five years. The couple were now considering divorce. As a result of information about the family that emerged in the first session, the trainee developed the following hypothesis consistent with being encouraged to take more of a position of authoritative doubt in formulating hypotheses.

"After five years of living separately, with B and J—the sons—spending time living with each parent, the mother (G) and father (S) are now moving towards divorce. During mediation discussions about divorce, G indicated that she intended to return to her country of origin after the divorce was completed, preferably with the children coming to live with her. At about the same time, the sons began refusing to go to school and 'acting out' with their mum. The father seems to have a sad and powerful story about his early life which resides within the shared family story, and it may be that this endows him with an element of vulnerability which precludes the boys acting out their confusion with him in the same way as they do with mother. In addition, the powerful conflictual relationship in which mother and father still very much appear to be engaged seems to dominate the family dialogue, and the children's voices are not strong enough to be heard. It may be that the impending divorce has resulted in the children acting out in order to keep the parents engaged with one another. Or it may be that the sons are school-refusing because of being bullied. In the same way, mother may want to go back to Eastern Europe to escape the conflict that she and her husband are caught up in and to seek the support of her family, or it may be that it is part of an ongoing power struggle between the two of them. The message I [the trainee therapist] perceive the husband to be giving me is, 'Please do let this woman take my children from me. Every family I have been part of has disintegrated.'"

One of the interesting aspects of this working hypothesis is that while, in the main, it concentrates on the family, the trainee is also beginning to hypothesize about the therapeutic relationship. As the training develops, trainees begin to become much more competent about developing this aspect of hypothesizing. In future sessions, for example, the hypothesizing went beyond only including the father. Recording in this way enables the supervisor to see clearly the development of skills being learned.

Main themes to emerge

One of the central tasks for a supervisor is to help trainees improve their abilities to elicit themes from content and to explore them through time, across relationships, and across contexts. The eliciting of themes not only relates to the content presented by clients, but also that presented by the therapeutic and supervisory systems per se. The headings in this section of the form also structure the trainee to adhere to a central systemic notion that we are always trying to explore different perceptions of reality.

Example

In relation to the W family mentioned in the hypothesizing section above, the themes to emerge for the clients were:

loyalty/disloyalty
trust/mistrust
protection/attack
safe/vulnerable
reliable/unreliable

For the trainee, the themes to emerge were:

"One son shows loyalty to mother's views, while one son shows loyalty to father's views. The children mirror the parents' polarized positions. I feel that each of the parents vies to present to me as the good parent and consequently to invite me to be loyal in the same way the children are."

For the other trainees and the supervisor behind the screen, one of the themes to emerge was whether the interviewer was being drawn more towards the vulnerability of the father than towards that of other members of the family and, if this was the case, why that might be so.

In relation to issues for supervision, the themes emerging above for the family, trainee, and those in the supervision team all contribute to issues for supervision to be recorded. But, in addition, and as part of the notion of reflecting processes (see below), I have since 1991 developed an exercise as part of the supervisory process which attempts to contribute to the supervisor becoming clearer about supervisory issues that may need addressing. Issues emerging then often become part of the recording process, not least in reflections by the consulting partner (see below).

Exercise: Addressing supervisory issues. The exercise usually takes place at the end of a supervision group session and depends on time available. I ask one of the four trainees in the group who has not interviewed in the clinic that day to interview me about my supervision of the group during that day's work together. Initially, the group members would have a brief session discussion alone before my being interviewed, but as people become more confident we do the interview without the trainees necessarily having a pre-discussion.

The exercise seems to be of use at a number of different levels. First, it helps me to take an observer perspective in relation to my own supervisory position. I am often asked, for example, "In your supervision of us today, is there anything, on reflection, that you would have preferred to have done differently." There might be questions related to gender—for example, "If you were a female supervisor, would it have made a difference to how you supervised John today in relation to such and such a family"—or, in relation to race and culture, I might be asked, "How did your thinking about working with mixed race couples influence your supervision of Jeanette [working with a mixed-race couple]." Even if it is uncomfortable at times for me, I can at least hold on to the view that I must be training them well! The concept of safe uncertainty applies to supervisors as well as to trainees.

Second, the exercise gives the message that the trainees can be helpful to me as well as my being helpful to them: that such practice within the supervisory system is another example of an overall supervisory approach consistent with the idea of mutual influence.

Third, the activity enables the trainees to be engaged in practising peer consultation to each other in addition to my supervising them in the framework of assessment. The exercise is an example of utilizing a collaborative approach within a hierarchical context.

End-of-session message or a summary of the reflecting-team discussion

The important issue to remember here is that it is not just the content that needs to be put down in the recording form, but some explanation as to why this particular message has been given or a further reflection on the reflecting-team discussion.

Theoretical concepts used

This section encourages the trainee to analyse his or her practice theoretically. It should not be a list of concepts. One or two concepts should be chosen and elaborated upon. Thus, the trainee might indicate that he or she was using a second-order perspective and highlight how this showed itself in practice in the session. The trainee might show this by illustrating the way he or she was developing a reflexive stance in the interviewing—for example, (to family members): "Thinking about how we are working together, what advice would you give me about the most useful direction we could go in for the rest of this meeting?"

Technique/skills used

This section is similar to the previous one, on theory, in that it should not just be a list of techniques. For example, the trainee may have used one or more reframes during the session: "Do you see your wife's anger more in terms of her disapproval of your point of view or more in terms of her possibly holding a new view, such as feeling more confident than she used to about your being able to handle a challenge?"

Issues pertaining to self

Since the late 1980s, the concept of self has become more prominent in the systemic field. Self had, for a long time, been mainly associated with psychodynamic psychotherapy and somehow did not belong to, or at the least was only marginally included in, the consideration of a systemic approach. However, the development in the late 1970s/early 1980s of a second-order perspective (Hoffman, 1985)—that reality was observer-dependent (Capra, 1982; Heisenberg, 1958), not observer-independent—in effect made it impossible any longer for systemic clinicians to refrain from incorporating self into their way of thinking. As Von Foerster (1990) has said, those who believed in the independent-observer position had "feared entering the forbidden land of looking at looking itself." He saw objectivity as "a device to avoid responsibility" (p. 5). As he further noted, we are not constructing reality, but what our relationship is with reality. In helping a trainee address his or her relationship with the reality of therapeutic and supervisory processes, we are encouraging the development of a systemic self—in particular, self-reflexivity (see Flaskas & Perlesz, 1996).

It is an important responsibility of the supervisor to help trainees recognize and understand patterns from within their own significant relationship system (past and present) and culture which may aid or constrain their clinical work (Burnham et al., 1996).

Example

In the earlier example of work with a couple in their 60s, a theme was elicited about fighting for survival. The trainee wrote in her record of the session how she had begun to think about the issues of fighting for survival and giving up and the relevance they have had in her own life. "There have been times when I have felt overwhelmed by events and circumstances and periods of not feeling up to the fight. However, for the most part these have usually been short lived. They happened when I was much younger, and I have come out fighting again. How do my own views about overcoming adversity help or hinder my work with this couple. Does it become harder to bounce back fighting as we age, or is that a prejudice that is preventing me from challenging this couple more than I am doing."

(The trainee shifted her practice to start taking more risks with the couple.)

I have noticed over the years of supervising that there appear to be a number of elements in the process of becoming more self-reflexive:

a. The recognition of the feeling/pattern—for example, "I am finding it difficult to go beyond safe conversation with this couple."

b. A connection with another context—for example, family-of-origin beliefs.
c. Reflections arising out of (a) and (b).
d. Actions consistent with the development of a different pattern in the therapy. (In taking action in the light of connections made, it is important here to make a distinction between the indirect utilization of self and the direct expression of self. In the former, the personal connection is not disclosed by the trainee in work with clients, whereas in the latter it is disclosed.)

More recently, I have begun to explore with supervisees the following related questions:

- "What issues/themes/feelings might you be pulling back from addressing in your work with clients/colleagues/wider systems?"
- "How do you explain to yourself why this process of 'pulling back from addressing' is occurring?"

These questions, of course, also apply to the supervisors themselves.

Such exploration is again part of a process of developing self-reflexivity. It is important to stress that the second question is not excluded or overlooked, for it invites the supervisee to explore explanation rather than only describe content.

Ethical issues

Attention to ethical matters in therapy should always be uppermost in the training process. It is thus important that the recording format should reflect this view. For example, in the work with the family mentioned in an earlier part of the chapter, there was concern that the children's voices mighty not be being heard. There was a good deal of discussion in the supervision group about informed consent and what ethical responsibility a therapist should take in ensuring that such an issue was addressed in the therapy.

Reflections on the writing-up of the interview

A day (at least) after writing up the record of the clinical interview, the trainee writes a brief reflection to further develop an observer perspective to his or her work.

Example

The following comes from notes relating to the first session with the W family:

"I've realized from writing up these notes that I really didn't develop a three-generational perspective in the session in order to get some sense of pattern through time and a clearer idea about themes that I could pursue. Perhaps this was inevitable, given the anxiety the parents had about making sure that I 'got all the facts', as they put it. I need to try and rectify this in the next session."

Reflections of the trainee's consulting partner

The consulting partnership is an idea devised by Ros Draper and John Hills (1992). In a supervision group of four trainees, there would be two pairs of consulting partnerships; these would be changed around after an agreed period of time. A consulting partnership is a peer consultation system. One of the benefits of such a partnership is that it contributes to the creation of a supportive context whereby trainees can be constructively challenging of each other. The partnership also helps the trainees become more competent at being commentators about each other's practice.

Example

"One of the things I am struck by when I read your record of the fourth session with the W family relates to the therapeutic relationship. I don't have a clear sense of your relationship to the family. I have a sense of the family feeling vulnerable about exposing themselves. How does it feel for you to be exposed in front of the team? I also have a sense that it is difficult for the family to trust connecting to one another, that it's safer to keep an emotional distance. How safe is it for you to connect with them?"

CONCLUSION

When the form is completed and the reflections returned, a copy of the whole recording form is sent to the supervisor, who then gives feedback to the trainee.

This structure becomes a central part of the supervisory relationship. It enables trainees to feel that they can receive detailed feedback about their progress and gives them a strong sense that they and their work are being given a great deal of attention. The benefit for supervisors is that they are enabled to see the progress of trainees at both an individual and a group level. If, for example, there seemed to be a pattern that hypothesizing was not very strong across the whole group, it would provide an opportunity for the supervisor and trainees to address how this was happening. It would also lead me, as a supervisor, to address whether I was contributing to this lack of progress by the way I was training the members of the group.

Initially, there was a feeling from trainees that filling in the form was a lot of work, and to some extent that feeling never disappears completely. However, the feedback from trainees over the last ten years has been almost unanimous in expressing the view that the format has helped them develop a rigour to their work—particularly in terms of theory, practice, the nature of change, and the therapeutic relationship—which they feel they may not otherwise have developed.

Acknowledgement. I would like to express my appreciation to the former trainees who have kindly allowed me to quote from their written recordings of sessions, particularly Lorraint Davies-Smith.

CHAPTER 4

Training systemic supervisors: multi-layered learning

Charlotte Burck & David Campbell

This chapter is about the way supervision can be conceptualized as a multi-layered system. It describes a framework for training which reflects the different levels of experience and different aspects of relationships involved in the supervisory process.

The family therapy supervision course is based in the Child and Family Department of the Tavistock Clinic, which is a large NHS clinic providing individual psychotherapy and family therapy trainings for a wide range of professional disciplines. The Tavistock established the first family therapy training in the U.K. in 1975. As the field has matured over the years, supervision has been taken more seriously as a crucial activity whose development must be given the same level of attention and conceptualization as the family therapy it is meant to foster. As long-standing trainers, we have been committed to the development of the field and therefore felt obliged and excited to develop a new level of training.

Three of us (Charlotte Burck, social worker; David Campbell, clinical psychologist; and Caroline Lindsey, child psychiatrist) set out to design a course to train systemic supervisors that would enable course members to learn the craft and theory of systemic supervision, and itself be systemic. Our aim has been to create a learning environment that would embody and reflect the systemic principles of context and feedback, in which both trainers and trainees would apply these systemic concepts and learn from systemic processes. In designing the training, we made great efforts to site the learning activities in distinctly different contexts and to track the way all of our thinking changed from one context to another. We also continually emphasized that learning new ideas and techniques was inseparable from the increased awareness of being part of a feedback process.

The chapter is structured in two sections. The first section describes the course and each of its components and the rationale for designing the course on the basis of systemic concepts. The second section discusses some of the training and supervision dilemmas and examines the impact of various stages of the training based on feedback from trainees. This is followed by a brief discussion by the authors.

OVERVIEW OF THE COURSE

The course runs over two years, meeting weekly in the first year and every three weeks in the second. The staff group of three rotate their contributions to the different aspects of the course to give the trainee supervisors the experience of their differences and to maximize different learning styles.

The course consists of five interlinking components and is designed to enable course participants to experience and reflect on various different aspects of systemic supervision. All trainee supervisors also do live supervision in their agency setting during the training programme.

The five components of the course are:

1. theory seminar
2. live supervision of live supervision
3. agency-based supervision seminar
4. personal/professional development seminar
5. observation of supervision groups.

Theory seminar

We think that it is important for trainees to be able to conceptualize clearly both about therapy and about supervision and to be knowledgeable about current debates in the family therapy field. We have needed to find a balance between exploring the literature about supervision and about developments in the systemic therapy field. With the field's move to the narrative approaches and ideas from social constructionism, it has been important to identify core systemic concepts that underpin therapy and supervision and explore how these can be applied within postmodern frameworks.

It has been useful to examine literature written decades apart that highlights assumptions, values and contexts, and the way issues of gender, racialization, culture, class, and sexual orientation have been developed, and to forefront issues of social justice and ethical dilemmas. A consideration of relevant research literature about families, family therapy, training and supervision, and its application in the supervision process is another important aspect of these seminars. As the supervision literature is sparse in comparison with family therapy literature generally, trainees too are encouraged to contribute papers for the seminar which they have found stimulating and relevant, and which relate to their own supervision dilemmas and agency contexts.

Over the years, we have organized the seminars in different ways, but we tend to ask trainees to briefly present a few key ideas from the papers that they feel are pertinent to our learning and our practice as supervisors, and this leads on to a fuller group discussion. Theory seminars frequently fall into the trap of becoming rarefied and divorced from practice, so we invite a shared responsibility for all to link the papers back to their own experiences on the course or in their agencies.

Live supervision of live supervision

Live supervision of live supervision takes place in a supervision group of three to four trainee supervisors plus one of the three staff members, who acts as the supervisor of the supervision. This takes place at the Tavistock Clinic with the families who are referred for therapy. Each of the trainee supervisors carries cases in which they act as supervisor to the therapist who is their colleague on the course; they also carry cases in which they act as therapist and are, in turn, supervised by another of their colleagues on the course. If a trainee is not in the role of supervisor or therapist, he or she will take the position of observer behind the screen. The staff member who is the live supervisor of the live supervision (LS of LS) facilitates the trainee supervisor's practice and enables reflection and feedback on these multi-layered experiences. The role of live supervisor is alternated among the staff members every half year by switching from one supervision group to another.

As trained therapists coming to acquire supervision skills, trainee supervisors are somewhat ill-prepared to find their own therapy under scrutiny once again. The task of fostering a context in which anxious trainee supervisors can supervise anxious but competent therapists in a helpful experimental way is crucial. We have found putting in place structures within the supervision of supervision groups has been useful to help keep boundaries of different subsystems clear, in what can easily be experienced as a recipe for muddle. It has been very helpful to use Milan-style formats of pre-session preparation of supervisor and therapist and mid- and end-of-session processing breaks. Following the feedback about the therapy, there are reflections about the supervisory processes from all the different perspectives—the therapist, the observer, the supervisor, and the supervisor of the supervision. This structure helps facilitate the development of self-reflexivity at all levels, which we in agreement with Burnham (1993) see as a primary aim in the training of supervisors as well as of therapists.

For trainee supervisors, a first shift involves focusing on the relationship between the therapist and the family and stepping back from trying to be a therapist behind the screen. The LS of LS needs to address the level of the supervisor–therapist relationship rather than slipping into supervisor role. Both need to find ways to keep in position while drawing on knowledge and experiences of being a therapist and a supervisor. The observer-member of the team is also able to pay attention to the relationship between the therapist and family, the supervisor and therapist, and the LS of

LS and the supervisor and to add comments and observations, particularly in the post-session debriefing.

The experience of mutuality created through the shifting of roles from therapist to supervisor to observer enhance the building of trust and the awareness of similar and idiosyncratic struggles. Experiencing interventions from the supervisor as a therapist and reflecting on their impact feeds directly into the experimentation with ways of positioning oneself as supervisor. The exploration of the intention and effect of the supervision with the LS of LS raises questions about therapy as well as supervision that reverberate across positions and sessions. Questions such as, "How can one best enhance a therapist's session and fit different ideas together to be usable?", are posed to both sides of the relationship. As LS of LS, we enable trainee supervisors to attend to the process of supervision—what are the effects of giving the therapist a plethora of ideas, of being over-respectful to the therapist's thinking, or of holding a very different belief from theirs? Questions to supervisors in the post-session reflections are also linked to personal/professional themes, with the aim of expanding self-reflexivity. These exchanges are further enriched through informal peer discussions as much as through other course components.

The transparent use of the LS of LS and of our own self-reflexivity has often become a marker in clarifying the appropriate levels of focus. Finding oneself responding as a supervisor rather than an as LS of LS and being able to reflect with the group about this experience can facilitate the supervisor's ability to do the same, as well as examining ideas such as the isomorphism of the relationships between family and therapist, therapist and supervisor, and supervisor and LS of LS (Liddle & Saba, 1983). The observer-member can also be helpful in the identification and reflections on these processes as someone in a different position. It is important for the LS of LS to create a context in which the observer is able to raise issues of this kind. A side-effect of training supervisors with this format has been that many of these professionals have also reconsidered their ideas about therapy, sometimes in unexpectedly profound ways.

Agency-based supervision seminar

Each trainee is required to provide ongoing supervision in his or her own or another agency to a professional wishing to develop his or her systemic therapy. Because trainees are also supervising their peers on the course, we have encouraged them to take on the supervision of colleagues with different levels of experience, as this provides a range of learning experiences for the group as a whole, with different challenges at different levels of experience. In their second year, trainees are asked to establish supervision groups, as learning to manage the group behind the screen is an essential—if further complicating—aspect of the supervision process. This experience develops skills in managing team dynamics and the use of an observing group in therapy (Roberts, 1989).

As in training therapists, we are convinced that learning family therapy supervision is greatly enhanced when parallel learning experiences are occurring in the work setting. This interweaving of the applications of ideas in different settings is particularly helpful in learning about the importance of the fit to context.

Since the supervisor in these settings often has a collegial relationship with the supervisee, there are complexities of relationships which must be negotiated at the outset and reviewed as the supervision continues. Questions of responsibility, boundaries, confidentiality, and hierarchy need to be discussed and clarified; the impact of the supervisory relationship on other relationships within the agency must also be considered. For example, we have had trainees supervising colleagues from other disciplines, and on one occasion the trainee was supervising her manager! The trainee supervisors make video recordings of their agency-based supervision sessions and present selections of dilemmas or issues they have identified for their own development in the supervision. These are discussed by the trainee group together with the supervisor of the agency supervision. We use these sessions to explore the personal struggle of the trainee to manage the role of supervisor and the interactive process between the supervisor and his or her supervisee. This component of the course is invaluable for understanding what supervision means in the context of an agency that has many tasks to fulfil and where a systemic framework may be one amid other therapeutic orientations.

For example, one issue explored in this setting is that of personal authority. Trainees often find it difficult to use their authority when supervising a colleague within their own staff group. One trainee dealt with this by becoming very "expert" and flooding the supervisee with more ideas than she could process. Another trainee was more diffident and found it very hard to say the things she was thinking about the therapy. Another challenge is the move from thinking only about the family (which is common practice in agency settings) to focusing on the development of the therapist, by discussing the personal meaning that a particular family may have for the therapist. In each situation, authority seemed easier to manage when the dual roles were discussed openly with the supervisee. Alongside the issues within the supervision process are the challenging questions of evaluation—both the evaluation of the supervision and the evaluation of the therapist's development and how best to facilitate this process (Storm et al., 1997).

Supervision of family therapy is an intensive experience, and it is easy to lose sight of the larger context, yet supervision will not be effective, let alone take place at all, if it is not carefully negotiated to fit into its working context. The trainees learn from comparing their experience at the Tavistock Clinic, which is a specialized training institution, with experiences "out there" in agencies that provide a more generalist service to clients. These seminars push the trainees to think at this level: they create a contextual level of observation, and by sharing experiences in the seminar each trainee is gathering a pool of contexts to learn from on the course.

Personal/professional development seminar

The personal/professional development (PPD) work on the course also focuses on multiple layers: the trainees' own PPD work as supervisors, how to do PPD work with the therapists they supervise (Hildebrand, 1998), and their curiosity about PPD issues for us as LS of LS. The decision to make the PPD work integral to the course rather than a self-contained module with an outside facilitator comes from our experience of the different relationship trainee supervisors have with the task of their self-development. The knowledge that they are already qualified and competent therapists seems to remove some of the anxiety sometimes attached to this work on family-therapy qualifying courses—for example, anxiety that difficult personal and family issues might somehow disqualify them from becoming therapists. Whatever the reason, trainee supervisors seem to approach the task of exploring personal issues for themselves as supervisors with somewhat more "freedom" than do trainee therapists. This does not, however, mean that there are no dilemmas or anxieties involved in the work. The identification of personal dilemmas that supervisors face related to their own family experiences is useful, as is a more narrative approach to their accounts of themselves as supervisors (cf. Clifton et al., 1990).

Explorations of difference and power are central to this module, particularly as some trainee supervisors will not have examined these issues adequately within their family therapy training. Developing a cultural sensitivity involves having one's own experiences, cultural identity, values and assumptions challenged and re-examined (CONFETTI, 1999; Hardy & Laszloffy, 1995). Elaborating how they as supervisors can work with meanings and across differences of gender, culture, racialized identity, class, and sexual orientation occurs through experiential exercises and role-plays (Burck & Daniel, 1995; CONFETTI, 1999).

These explorations are linked both to their supervision on the course and in the agency, attempting always to include wider contextual concerns. The ability to link PPD learning to the other aspects of the course has convinced us of the importance of our own involvement in it.

Alongside their own personal explorations, supervisors also develop ideas to help therapists explore personal resonances to their work (Lindsey, 1993). This is a particularly challenging issue in agency supervision, where this aspect of supervision is often new territory. Therefore, negotiating permission to do so is the initial task—that is, clarifying the objectives of enhancing the therapist's competence, as well as taking up issues of confidentiality and boundary keeping in their relationships outside the supervision context.

Beginning to ask therapists about personal connections to particular families has often been experienced as daunting. However, the experience of being able to develop questions for therapists at this level and the experience of how helpful this can be provides a powerful rationale to develop this further. The discussions of their own and each other's personal development within the course also powerfully influences the ways they develop this work in their agency supervision.

Trainee supervisors are often very interested to explore with tutors how they themselves use personal resonances in a reflexive way, and they ask questions about how and on what occasions a supervisor can use self-disclosure. This has pushed our own development as supervisors and trainers in clarifying use of self in the supervision task.

Observation of supervision groups

In order to provide the trainees with another level of supervision experiences, we arrange for the trainee group to observe live supervision groups conducted either by the tutors or by other experienced family therapy supervisors who are providing supervision on other courses within the Child and Family Department at the Tavistock—for example, the supervision groups on the family-therapy qualifying Master's course.

The observations are structured in the following way: two or more of the supervision-course trainees sit silently behind the one-way mirror observing the supervisor, who is supervising live work with two or three other group members behind the screen. They will see the supervisor relating to the therapist and engaging the other group members in relevant discussion, and then summarizing the whole process with the group at the end. When this has been completed, the supervision-course trainees are able to interview the supervisor, the therapist, and observers about the process.

We describe this as an opportunity to learn more about different styles of supervision and their effects upon the therapist, the family, and the observers. From a conceptual point of view, the trainees take a more distant observer position from the one they take within their own course team, and this position allows them to formulate different hypotheses about what may be going on. They also have the opportunity to pursue their ideas by interviewing and getting direct feedback from all those involved. Each individual and each sub-group within the system can be quizzed about how the process affected them.

The trainees ask such questions as: (to the supervisor) "What was your intention when you telephoned that message to the therapist?" or "Can you explain why you are using different styles of supervision with each therapist you supervised today?" or (to the therapist) "How helpful was it for you in the post-session discussion today when the supervisor made that comment that you needed to stay connected to the family's affect?" or (to the observer) "Has it been clear to you today why the therapist suggested that the marital conflict should not be taken up?"

We try to create many opportunities for the trainees both to place themselves in different positions within the overall supervisory process and, perhaps most importantly, to generate feedback that gives meaning to the aspect of supervision they are observing and experiencing. From the tutor's point of view, the experience of being interviewed about our own supervision style has proved illuminating. The questions we are asked can be challenging and unsettling, forcing us to probe more deeply into the rationale for our actions and, as a result, making us more aware of what we are doing—or think we are doing—when we supervise.

PERSPECTIVES ON THE COURSE

To enable the reader to experience what this course is like for the participants, we now revisit the components of the course from the perspective of the participants. This section discusses the course as it has been experienced, illustrating the discussion with quotations from trainees following the completion of the course.

Live supervision of live supervision

The part of the course involving live supervision of live supervision, set up for trainees to learn to supervise each other and to experience their peers' supervision of themselves as therapists, functioned as the "hot-house" or "sweat-box" of the course—the laboratory in which all experiences were open to reflection.

The first assumption of the trainee supervisors to be faced was that, as qualified therapists, they did not need to learn anything more as therapists: alongside this was acute anxiety about being observed and possibly found wanting by someone who had been given the task to help them think not only about the family and their therapy, but also about their ongoing development as therapists. This engendered much of the unsettledness at the beginning of the training. None of these trainee supervisors had come on the course to have their therapeutic skills further developed.

The structure of both supervising and being supervised meant that each person had to think carefully about his or her own theoretical position as a therapist and how he or she might translate some of that knowledge into being able to help a therapist who came with a different orientation. Although we were known as a staff group who had taught a Milan and post-Milan systemic therapy course in the past, we had attracted therapists wishing to train as supervisors who were influenced by different theoretical ideas including structural, Bowenian, and strategic family therapy, the narrative approaches as well as attachment theory.

The trainees' first experiences of supervising each other and being supervised were characterized by extreme politeness and rather tentative learning about the other's position. Unsettling effects of feeling de-skilled, as well as a tension between the said and the unsaid in supervision, were experienced—if not, perhaps, always being part of the conversation from the first first. As one trainee described this,

> "Initially I found my partner extremely competent but defensive and denying that he had any difficulty with being supervised by a total stranger. This was not unreasonable—I think I knew how he felt."

Eventually these aspects of the supervision experience became part of the ongoing discussions in the training group, as the group became less preoccupied by performance anxiety and more interested in process:

> "I decided to treat our relationship in terms of process—i.e. that hopefully it would develop and relax as we worked together."

As one of the trainees summarized this experience later:

> "Organized by the level of expertise and experience of my colleagues . . . initially I tended to be over-respectful. Getting the balance between respect for another's ability and different style while having sufficient confidence in one's own expertise and being confident enough to share it in an enabling way is one of the most complex aspects of supervision."

To maximize the trainees' learning about their own learning as supervisors and their peers' learning style as therapists, we ask them to prepare mid-year handover reports at the point where the supervisory arrangements change over. These reports comment on their supervisor and their supervisee and are a more formal opportunity for mutual evaluation. This enabled a grappling with the challenging issue of evaluation and how to manage this in collaborative ways (Storm et al., 1997). For those working in pairs, supervising each other, the co-evolving and interactive nature of this was highlighted, with a mutual struggle to open up to new ideas and face challenges to cherished approaches.

Issues of cloning and ideas about isomorphism (Liddle & Saba, 1983) were examined as they bumped up against having to work across different theoretical models. The therapists' different styles and different theoretical influences sparked some interesting mutual re-evaluations of their own beliefs about therapy. The supervision task eventually was constructed by this group as "helping each other build a personal way of constructing their own practice".

As supervisors of the live supervision, we also had to work hard to find the most enabling position to take up. Initially, our giving input only at the level of the supervisor's interventions led the trainees to ask for more contribution of our ideas at all levels of the supervisory system. In some ways, our struggle to find the right position mirrored some of their own dilemmas as supervisors, although they tended initially to find themselves mostly preoccupied by the family in therapy, which often gave them the most problems about how to use their ideas helpfully. This became less of an issue as they were able to pay more attention to the level of the therapist's relationship with the family and their relationship with the therapist, as well as their own position.

Learning about each other's learning styles and getting feedback about their own learning process were also crucial elements in the supervision process which were clarified in this "laboratory" as well as in the PPD slot. For example, one trainee described how helpful it was to learn that his partner's need to debate ideas with him behind the screen was his way of being able to make use of them in the room with the family, rather than not finding his ideas useful which was how he had experienced this initially. Another trainee noticed that the therapist she supervised found her questions about his therapy intimidating; she found a way to make her own thinking more explicit and transparent and then engage him in discussion about how this might help or not with his own dilemmas as therapist.

Several themes emerged repeatedly during the course. A phrase that became a watchword for one of the trainees was: "Just keep talking about the complexities in the relationship." We also engendered complexity through the change of staff roles and supervisory pairs with the idea that these differences would maximize learning and unsettle an idea about one right way to supervise.

Addressing differences of gender, racialized identities, and culture within the supervising team accompanied and enhanced the examination of power and hierarchy in the supervision and therapy process. All three staff members are white. Our first training group consisted of four people: two women, two men; three white, one black; two British, one African, one Australian. It was useful to examine the constraints to challenging across differences of "race" and culture, highlighting the influence of the wider context of disrespect, disqualification, and racism as well as personal contexts, to enable ways to challenge respectfully across differences. This group of trainees noted that they experienced more conflict when working in cross-gendered partnerships than in same-gendered pairings, and that there were considerable differences in the way the female and male pairs worked. The switch from a male supervisor to a female supervisor halfway through the year also had its effect, with the male trainees feeling more supported by David Campbell and the female trainees by Charlotte Burck. These reflections allowed further unpacking of gendered difference and how this might be explored in supervision and therapy.

The issue of the "unsaid" in supervision came to the fore in relation to ideas about hidden agendas and indirectness. This sometimes resulted in the experiences such as the following one, reported by one trainee about the supervisor: "On a few occasions his questions have seemed a bit ambiguous, leaving me wondering what message he was trying to get through to me."

Issues of responsibility were also of interest: who was holding it, when, and with what effect on all the participants' thinking and acting? Initially, feelings of responsibility on the part of the supervisor sometimes led to an experience of paralysis or acute performance anxiety. One trainee commented on how she realized that she needed to move from taking responsibility for the session, through identifying moments when she moved to becoming directive (such as when she felt that a therapist lost focus), to becoming more curious about her own anxieties. This move to seeing oneself as a resource rather than as responsible was one of the transformative leaps in this trainee supervisor's learning. These kinds of leaps were often accompanied by a growing ability to rely on learning from the supervision process itself.

Helping the trainee supervisors find a useful framework with which to think about their therapists' development was a primary task for us as supervisors of the supervision. Here the idea about identifying dilemmas for the therapist in relation to the family's issues seemed a useful one. Other questions we have posed that seem to have been particularly helpful for trainee supervisors include the following:

- What is the therapist trying to create with the family?
- What is the family trying to create with the therapist?
- What story of themselves as a family are the family trying to create?
- What story of herself/himself as a therapist is the therapist trying to create?
- What are the therapist's main dilemmas?

On the whole, the trainee supervisors moved from over-respectfulness to becoming more challenging and from questioning the therapist about his or her thinking to a more balanced position of both adding their own ideas and helping the therapist formulate his or her own. Being able to ask for and receive direct feedback from the therapist has been one of the most crucial learning points.

> "The process of interviewing colleagues about my live supervision helped. . . . The whole experience 'desensitized' me to my fear of asking. I know much better now that what I offer is usually found useful, but not always. That makes it important to ask."

Observation of us as supervisors of trainee therapists

One of the most important learning contexts of the course for us as staff has been the trainees' observation of the live supervision that we do on the family therapy qualifying Master's course. Like many other trainers, there have few contexts in which to think about our supervision explicitly and in ongoing ways. Indeed, many of the current family therapy supervisors in Britain learned supervision initially by doing it, rather than going through a formal supervision training. This meant that much of our theory and practice of supervision has remained implicit. The interviews by the pairs of trainee supervisors following their observation of our supervision brought to our attention aspects of our practice which we ourselves had not noticed and forced us to clarify our theoretical underpinnings.

The trainees themselves considered these observations a good learning experience and said that they were particularly interested to see how the supervisors handled difficult moments. So, for example, if the therapist began to feel irritated with the family or particular members of the family, they were struck by the way a supervisor would track these feelings with the therapist to try to discover the context of beliefs or experiences which informed them, in order to help the therapist take a different position in the room with the family. Issues of pace and timing were also raised, as some supervisors were more interventive more often, whereas others bided their time.

Supervision of agency supervision

The experiences of agency supervision brought home different constraints to consider and how ideas might need to be applied differently in the agency context. We had made a decision to have the trainee supervisors supervise someone in their agency at different levels of experience, including those newer to systemic ideas. This meant that there were many experiences to unpack about how to work with therapists' different belief systems about change and therapy.

One trainee had contracted to supervise a colleague who was very experienced in her own field and new to systemic ideas. A major organizing factor to the supervision process became this professional's dislike of asking questions outside a problem-solving model, as she considered this to be voyeuristic. The trainee supervisor's work included unsettling this idea through considering which levels of the situation might impact on the present interactions and helping the therapist to ask about a wider context, which families then reported was helpful. Here, the supervisor together with the family were able to change this therapist's relationship to what was relevant to therapy.

Trainees have commented on how much they have learned from and about the complexities of families and therapy, as much as about supervision:

"I feel that I am expanding my options for conceptualizing frameworks for making sense of complex family problem presentations. This enables me to help a supervisee expand their hypotheses about a case."

Other dilemmas that we struggled with were: (1) How to note positive change with a therapist who is always down-playing herself, without this becoming a symmetrical loop. (2) How to open up conversations about difference as a black supervisor with a white therapist working with a black family, and as a white supervisor with a black therapist working with a white family, which challenges constraint and idealization—how to enable a use of similarities to join and begin the work when there is a paralysis around issues of difference, and then return to discuss some of the complexities around differences and power. (3) How to manage one's critical side without either becoming a "closet dictator" or giving up on one's critical edge.

Personal/professional development

"What an intimate business supervision is."

These personal/professional development sessions are devoted to considering personal resonances to the supervision task. Initially, trainees revisit the ways in which they themselves had been supervised and the effect this had had on their beliefs about supervision. Exploring their ideas about the differences between themselves as therapists and as supervisors has also been useful to unpack beliefs about supervision further.

Examining their own professional and educational scripts has led to thinking about how they can explore these with the therapists they supervise and use it explicitly as part of the supervision process, as well as find ways to attain a fit with their therapists' learning style.

Identifying particular themes in their supervision to explore in these seminars has also been critical to their learning. Issues of responsibility and authority have been central, and exploring these in the context of family of origin and previous professional experiences has helped trainee supervisors to take different positions in their supervising.

At other times, it was the noting of significant moments in their experiences on the course—as observers, as therapists, or as supervisors—which became significant turning points in their learning and practice as supervisors. One trainee noted that being helped to stay with a dilemma beyond the point when she would have usually been diverted was significant for herself both as therapist and as supervisor working with other therapists; for another trainee, watching a supervisor able to work with a trainee's strength in the face of therapy not going well, which helped the trainee work with the mother in the family in the face of family life not going well, became an enabling way out of an overly critical position.

Central, then, to the learning process is how trainee supervisors come to realize the importance of paying attention to the way "the personal histories of supervisor and supervisee can facilitate or obstruct the supervision process".

Developing self-reflexivity

One of our main aims on the course has been the development of the self-reflexivity (Burnham, 1993) of the supervisors we are training, and the course has also demanded this of us as trainers and supervisors of supervisors. Setting up a context in which we could mutually examine the various aspects of supervision has meant that we ourselves have had to take up a stance as learners, to be responsive to feedback, and to be involved in re-examining our own beliefs and experiences of supervision, while at the same time being able to communicate some certainties about what we have found helpful in the supervision process. This has required a certain level of risk-taking as teaching staff, able to be transparent about our own learning processes in the various positions we take up in the course and to examine the differences between us. It may be that it was when we first designed the course that we were at our most transparent about our own learning—the course as laboratory for ourselves, as well as the trainee supervisors, as we set out to evaluate together all aspects of the course to develop further the opportunities for mutual learning. It is this aspect of the course and our self-reflexivity as trainers we most want to develop further, alongside our grasp of the complexities involved in the many-layered systems in which the family, the therapist, and the supervisor are embedded.

DISCUSSION

Confidence grows with time. With the experience of several cohorts going through the training, we now have considerable faith that the structures that we have set up bring forth processes that enable learning about supervision, and this has allowed us to think more carefully about supervision and supervisory relationships.

Live supervision is the most challenging way to supervise. A supervisor has to be on his or her toes continually, keeping an eye on all the different relationships and levels, often confronted by the unexpected, and knowing that he or she has to make decisions. Like therapy, live supervision has its thrilling moments, its boring moments, and its excruciating ones. Learning to make use of these involves not only having a clear framework with which to consider the multi-layers of the supervisory system and a range of techniques to gain manoeuvrability as a supervisor, but also being able to hold one's nerve and make space to reflect on one's own position.

Just as we as trainers are now more able to sit back and observe the developing relationship between the supervisor and the therapist, so the supervisors learn to observe the relationship between the therapist and the family.

Good supervision, like good therapy, has a lot to do with making good connections, developing an empathic relationship with what the supervisee is feeling and thinking and trying to achieve in the therapy. We try to identify the ideas, values and experiences that connect the supervisor and therapist—and those that push them apart so that they struggle to stay "on the same wavelength". Too much similarity or too much difference provides challenges for the supervisor.

Supervisors can sometimes be preoccupied with their own sense of anxiety and responsibility about their performance or their excitement about particular ideas, and this may hinder their ability to tune into the therapist's preoccupations. We watch for comments or questions that are not taken up. For example, during a pre-session discussion, the supervisor suggested framing a family member's behaviour in positive terms, but it seemed as though the therapist wasn't listening, because she didn't respond. When we discussed this later, it became apparent that rather than wanting new ideas about the forthcoming session, she needed support for her own anxieties about it. This led to a discussion about how a supervisor can elicit the therapist's preoccupations and anxieties, can empathize with their state. At other times, the supervisor and therapist may hold very different ideas about the way the therapy should be conducted, and this can be experienced as an impasse. We have generated ideas about how a supervisor can maintain a sense of some manoeuvrability at such moments, such as unpacking these ideological and theoretical differences and locating them in relation to other contexts to move things forward, or being able to step out of the engagement in the difference to think about this at another level—for example, what this might mean in relation to polarizations in other relationships in this multi-levelled system.

Training in supervision highlights personal relationships to evaluation, and in particular to criticism. Trying to find a balance between the wish to demonstrate competence and the ability to take on new ideas is complicated, whether as a therapist being supervised, as a trainee supervisor or as a trainer of supervisors. Will we be found wanting? Does a new idea disqualify our previous practice? As our course is built on the principle of observed practice at all levels, all of us are mutually under observation (although some of us are more powerful than others). Working to build relationships of trust takes time and comes partly through the experience of mutuality of sensitivity to criticism, and the building of respect for each other's perspectives. We need the support of each other and mutual respect to be able to take the risks of giving negative, as well as positive, feedback and to be open about competitiveness, fears, and differences. We have learned that it can often take up to half of the first year before the trainees feel comfortable enough with each other and with us to take these risks

It takes time for trainees to develop their own authority, to be able to assert their point of view. This process includes becoming confident that they can offer a helpful perspective. Sometimes this is by virtue of the supervisor's different position in the system, being able to observe the relationship between the therapist and family. Sometimes it comes from a supervisor's ideas about the family and the therapy. At other times, it is the supervisor's faith that the process of conversation with the therapist—the way they conduct this conversation—will generate helpful ideas for the therapy. Alongside this, supervisors need to find ways to introduce ideas to therapists who have different learning styles, sometimes introducing ideas through questions, sometimes laying them alongside the therapist's ideas for debate, sometimes focusing on one idea more directly. These distinctions between different ways to be authoritative as a supervisor create a context in which trainee supervisors do not have to be experts or even have more experience as therapists, and certainly not feel they have to have the "right" answer, but do take responsibility for taking charge of the process of supervision. Learning to be authoritative in relation to uncertainty is also a challenge. One trainee said that he had managed to say to the supervisee: "I'm not sure how this is going to turn out, but I want you to say to the father, 'The family needs you to be around more.'" The trainee used his authority even though he was uncertain about the outcome of his intervention and was able to say so. We talk on the course about how to be authoritative yet stay open for further discussion and other points of view. We also discuss trainees' ability to own the authority that is vested in the position of supervisor by those who enter the supervisory relationship and therefore to utilize its potential for learning.

However, there is another important aspect to the supervisor's authority, and that is: who holds responsibility for the outcome of the therapist's work? Our course is based in an NHS clinic, and the final responsibility in this case lies not with the trainee supervisor but with the staff member acting as LS of LS. But our trainees also work in other settings, and it has been crucial for the development of the relationship that both supervisor and supervisee know the range and limit of the supervisor's responsibility. When this is clear, it seems to smooth the path for claiming supervisory authority.

And last, but not least, it is often the families who provide the feedback that makes the difference to the therapist when trying out new ideas provided by the supervisor. Process and outcome studies, which include the families' perspectives on the therapy they receive as part of the training of supervisors, are crucially needed to continue to elaborate the significant processes and incidents that make up good effective therapy and supervision.

CONCLUSION

We have tried to maintain some balance between, on the one hand, holding to our own views and course structures long enough for them to have an impact on the trainees' learning (a positioned authority which we know is contingent), and, on the other, shifting our thinking in response to the feedback from trainees. After agonizing for some time about this, we have arrived at the position of sharing this balancing act with the trainees, so all of us can take responsibility for giving feedback at a higher level of complexity. This is similar to our experience with the inevitably vexing issue of hierarchy. We have learned both to build the structures that allow trainees to experience hierarchy in many contexts and to provide sufficient time to talk about it. Finally, as trainers, this course has reinforced our intention to learn and develop our own practice and thinking. We believe that collaborative relationships between trainers and trainees work best when trainers are genuinely coming to learn—but it is not always easy to maintain that positioning.

Acknowledgements. The trainees who have helped us close the feedback loop are the past and present members of the supervision training course: Peter Attwood, Jenny Brown, Matthew Ganda, Vicki Bianco, Enid Colmer, Olivera Markovic, Linda McCann, Percy Aggett, Paul Fletcher, Collette Richardson, Mike Vine, Ros Walker, Lynn Willis.

CHAPTER 5

The interlocking of therapy and supervision: the Athenian experience from the viewpoint of supervisors and supervisees

Vlassis Tomaras & Valeria Pomini

In their definition of supervision, all systemic therapists would include its interactional aspect. The development of supervision and/or training presupposes the creation of a co-evolving system between supervisors/trainers and supervisees/trainees (Campbell, Draper, & Huffington, 1988). Since the theoretical underpinning of family therapy supervision has been criticized as inadequate (Everett & Koerpel, 1986), some classificatory remarks on the supervision process, in general, could be adopted. Hawkins and Shohet (1989), for instance, have divided all supervisory activities into the therapy system (content, strategies, and therapeutic relationship) and the supervisory system (the therapist's "transference", the supervisor's "countertransference", and the here-and-now issues between them). It is stressed that patterns pertaining to these two systems are isomorphic (Haley, 1976; Liddle & Schwartz, 1983).

Apart from the conceptual framework of systemic supervision, its implementation embraces various methods and techniques that, to a great extent, depend on: (1) the theoretical orientation of the supervisors and (2) the context in which supervision is delivered. The term "supervision" is often used with different meanings, and for describing different activities in the systemic field. Supervision may denote, for instance, an external consultation to a depleted therapist (White, 1997), where the therapist uses the outsider to externalize his or her inner process (Rober, 1999); or, it may be addressed to a team of professionals/therapists who find themselves in uncertainty or in stressful situations (Shamai, 1998). In addition, supervision can be perceived as embedded in the framework of training (Boscolo, Cecchin, Hoffman, & Penn, 1987; De Bernart & Dobrowolski, 1996).

Our presentation aims to describe a tentative methodology for constructing a reflexive supervisory system within a certain socio-cultural and organizational context. We conceptualize reflexivity as a continuous recursive process involving supervisors and supervisees.

The setting

The University Mental Health Research Institute, Athens, provides training in systemic family therapy via a four-year course. The training schedule comprises 600 hours altogether, allocated to family sessions, supervision, and theoretical seminars. The trainees, mostly psychiatrists and clinical psychologists, undertake therapeutic responsibility, during the last two years of the course, by seeing at least six families and couples, either as therapists or by sharing therapeutic responsibility as co-therapists. Supervision is mainly provided by the two authors/organizing tutors, who are assisted by a third colleague. In addition, consultant-supervisors from abroad are regularly invited.

Therapy is delivered at the premises of the family and marital therapy clinic belonging to the psychiatric hospital of the Athens University Medical School. The two senior family therapists (i.e. the authors) have come to adopt a rather flexible systemic–integrative paradigm, which allows for a variety of therapeutic approaches. It is worth mentioning that they hold entire clinical responsibility for all cases referred.

The dyad of senior therapists/trainers/supervisors had to elaborate their differences (VP, a woman, psychologist, Italian/

non-acculturated, without academic post, trained by Boscolo and Cecchin at the Milan Centre of Family Therapy; VT, a man, psychiatrist, Greek, with academic status, trained at the Maudsley Hospital, London). At the outset of their working partnership, they thought of their differences, if enacted, as jeopardizing the therapeutic outcome or the cohesion of the group. Gradually they allowed themselves to expose their diverse or even contrasting views, attitudes, and so forth in front of the clients, usually in a reflecting-team form. By this practice they noticed that families felt comfortable to disclose themselves, and the therapeutic dialogue was promoted. Moreover, the trainees seemed to be more confident and to take initiative.

From the very beginning of their venture, the dyad (VP–VT) considered themselves part of a system containing four components: their agency(ies), the clients, the trainees, and themselves. They were expected to respond to the feedback given by the other three components, but there is a question as to how equally they did respond. Retrospectively reflecting on this issue, we assume that the response to the needs and expectations of the other parts fell into a pattern in which the trainees were left behind. Yet, as the training continued, the dyad became less directive and more suggestive, whether in therapy or in training, and the trainees became more competent and less compliant. Could this drift not influence all levels of activities—that is, therapy, training, and supervision?

Modes of supervision

Supervision in live sessions

All trainees have been exposed to four types of live supervision.

1. The trainee therapist meets the family, and the supervisor stays behind the screen.
2. The supervisor and the trainee therapist enter the room as co-therapists.
3. Two trainees act as co-therapists, and the supervisor stays behind the screen.

4. The supervisor and a trainee therapist enter the room as co-therapists, while another trainee stays behind the screen and is assigned the role of supervisor.

From the viewpoint of supervisors, Modes 3 and 4 are preferable as economizing time and staff. Mode 4 is considered as particularly advantageous because a reserved trainee/co-therapist is prompted to a more active therapeutic role by his or her partner—that is, the senior therapist—while at the same time another trainee is experiencing, behind the screen, the complexity of the supervisory role. For these reasons the supervisors decided to give more space to this mode; the tendency now is for the majority of our live supervisory events to take place under the latter scheme.

"Supplementary" supervision

Another four types of supervision, disconnected from live family therapy sessions, are also being practised. The trainees are exposed to all four types:

1. The trainee is individually supervised on videotaped sessions. A second trainee participates if he or she was involved in the live therapy.
2. There is group supervision of videotaped sessions. In this case, the supervisor and the group of trainees co-supervise.
3. The group supervises cases presented by the trainees; they bring their notes or videotaped material from sessions conducted in their own facilities.
4. Group supervision with invited consultants takes place, usually in a "marathon" format—that is, in an all-day supervisory session.

The supervisors arbitrarily chose to define the non-live supervision as "supplementary", probably influenced by the tenet prevailing at the time of their own training—namely, that live supervision is the strongest tool for training family therapists (Haley,

1976). Comparing the sub-types of the latter mode of supervision, the dyad felt more comfortable with group supervision—that is, in sharing the supervision job with all members of the group. Inevitably, group dynamics develop in the process of group sessions, and it is a difficult issue for the supervisors as to how far they allow them to proceed, or to be worked through. On the other hand, they see individual video-supervision sessions as a unique opportunity for a *tête-à-tête* encounter with the trainee in which his or her weak aspects can be discussed and his or her interviewing skills can be boosted. Weak aspects of the supervisor–supervisee relationship can be discussed within the same context.

Feedback from the graduates

The supervisors hold the view that the structure and process of their training course is flexible and permeable, thanks to a feedback loop involving them and the trainees/supervisees. Although their view is based upon the everyday information provided by the supervisees throughout the training course, it also reflects their own constructions and prejudices. How could the supervisees have the chance to evaluate their training/supervisory system in a more formal and valid way?

With this purpose in mind, the dyad of supervisors constructed a questionnaire and administered it to a group of fourteen trainees at the end of their training (1994–1998). The characteristics of the group were as follows: mean age 39.6 years; eight females, six males; four psychiatrists and child psychiatrists, nine psychologists, one social worker. The group was asked to compare all types of supervision they had experienced, by means of three questions: "Which type is the most useful for you?" "Which type is the most difficult for you (i.e. which is the most demanding, hard to implement, and provoking of discomfort)?" "Which one do you prefer?"

Regarding live supervision, the majority of respondents marked Mode 1 (the trainee with the family, the supervisor behind the screen) as the most difficult and Mode 4 (the supervisor and the trainee as co-therapists) as the preferable one. Concerning "supplementary" supervision, the answers were more or less equally distributed among its four types. The comparison of individual to group supervision showed that the former was considered as more difficult and more useful (10 out of 14), although the latter was preferred (10 out of 14). The supervisors' interpretation of this finding is that individual supervision asks the trainee for more therapeutic responsibility and prompts him or her to brainstorm. In group supervision, instead, responsibility is shared among the group members, who feel more relaxed and supported by each other.

Live as compared to "supplementary" supervision did not significantly differ in terms of usefulness, difficulty, and preference.

Another section of the questionnaire elicited responses interesting enough to be quoted verbatim:

During supervision, the supervisor places emphasis on:

A. How you handle the intra-familial dynamics.
B. Your relationship with the family (family/therapist dynamics)
C. Your own constructions which may affect your attitudes towards the family, and your interventions.

	A	B	C
Which one is more useful for you?	4	7	3
Which one is more difficult for you?	0	2	12
Which one do you prefer?	5	7	2

Three more questions from the same section are of note:

(a) Does your relationship with your supervisor affect the family session you conduct?

Eleven replied "yes", the rest replied "yes, somewhat".

(b) Do you find it useful to discuss with your supervisor about how you relate to each other in the procedure of therapy and supervision?

Ten replied "yes", the rest replied "rather yes".

(c) Suppose that it is feasible, during supervision, for an external supervisor to observe and comment on your relationship with your own supervisor. Would it be useful for you?

Eleven replied "yes", two replied "yes, somewhat", and just one replied "no" or "no, somewhat".

Here was a clear message to be received by the supervisors: they should pay more attention to the supervisor–supervisee relationship, as it develops within therapy and supervision. Eventually, the whole questionnaire was able to reveal information that was extensively discussed with the group of graduates. Moreover, it served as an input to the planning of the training course for a new group of beginners.

Tracing the novices' expectations and attitudes

At the time the previous group was completing the four-year training course, a new group was starting the same course. This group consisted of sixteen trainees, aged 34 years on average. Females outnumbered males (11 vs 5); half of them were psychiatrists or child psychiatrists, and the other half clinical psychologists (8 vs. 8).

Initiating this new cycle of training, the dyad (VP–VT) felt ready to introduce organizational modifications based on the feedback from the graduates, but also on information gathered from the beginners. A questionnaire was created to trace expectations and attitudes and was given to the novices. Two questions were considered as pivotal by the dyad:

(a) What should the supervisor's role be when you start seeing families?

Only three replied "teach me his/her approach and techniques". Another seven chose the answer "allow me to retain and use whatever suits me". The remaining six judged the latter answer as suitable for the advanced stages of the training.

(b) What should the supervisor's role be during the sessions?

Only five respondents looked forward to guidance; the others wanted to take the initiative themselves and their supervisor to comment after the session.

A considerable part of this questionnaire was devoted to gender and power issues, as the supervisors had found that these issues obstructed therapy in the past and produced tension among trainees or between a trainee and a supervisor. Two vignettes that were incorporated in the questionnaire are quoted here.

A. While you are seeing a couple, the wife turns to you and says: "I believe that a married man has the right to go out with others, and even stray at times, as long as he doesn't ruin his marriage and is ok within his family. What do you think?"

B. While you are seeing a couple, the husband turns to you and says: "All that women's rights and lib stuff is nonsense . . . the man is always in charge, and if he lashes out at times, well, it's not such a big deal . . . these things can be worked out in a family . . . I don't know, do you have a different opinion?"

The following was added to both vignettes:

The wife's/husband's statement

- aggravates you ☐
- annoys you to some extent ☐
- you are emotionally neutral ☐

At the same time she/he asks for your opinion. What would your first response be? (say something, stay silent, dodge the question, etc.). Specify.

Noticeably, nine respondents declared emotional neutrality in the first vignette; however, only four stated neutrality in the second vignette, where violence is concerned. Regarding the open question tracing their response, it was fortunate that only a few respondents (4 in the first, 2 in the second vignette) replied "I would stay silent" or "I would refuse to answer". Needless to say, all answers to the questionnaire varied according to the gender of the trainees: female trainees were more prone than were their male counterparts to react emotionally and to confront the sexist statements.

In a subsequent group session, all responses to the questionnaire were presented by the dyad and were discussed with the novice trainees. It seems that this resulted in increasing awareness of their attitudes, prejudices, and so forth and of their potential role in therapy. Nonetheless, the supervisors became aware of their trainees' vulnerabilities and of their own contribution in overcoming them.

COMMENTS

Feedback, with its continuous flow, facilitates changes in all levels of the therapeutic–training–supervisory system, including in the therapeutic and the supervisory relationships. Changes in all the sub-systems occur more or less in parallel, but they cannot go beyond the structural and organizational limits of the whole system. The art of drawing feedback from the trainees/supervisees requires sensitivity on the part of trainers/supervisors, but some techniques maybe helpful. Questionnaires provided at different stages of training are expected to prove useful tools for this purpose.

Most of our trainees do find that a scheme of an external supervision is useful for their clinical practice. However, it is clear from our study that the graduates prefer their supervisor to give priority to the therapeutic and supervisory relationships instead of the particular therapeutic techniques in which they have been schooled. Also, they find it difficult in supervision to elaborate their shortcomings in therapy, especially if this is going to bring up their personal or family experiences. Could it be that they feel fed up with hearing about interviewing skills, techniques of family therapy, and so forth? Might our initial expectation to prepare competent family therapists be (consciously or subconsciously) a "missionary" intention? In any case, we feel it necessary to focus more on the supervisory relationship, but on the contractual basis that the supervisory relationship is concentrated around the here-and-now of the shared clinical practice. In addition, to respect the trainees/supervisees' wish not to disclose themselves, we should refrain from "analysing" them.

It is not remarkable that the novice trainees ask for more autonomy and less guidance in therapy. This possibly reflects the contemporary epistemological and ideological trends in the systemic field, and/or it is related to their supervisors' attitudinal shifts in teaching, training, and relating to them. Their expectations call for adaptation to a more egalitarian and co-creative training and supervisory context.

Furthermore, the supervisors had to take into account that their groups of trainees/supervisees are not homogeneous, and to extensively discuss this issue. The trainees are quite dissimilar as to professional status, job description, psychotherapeutic background, idiosyncrasy, and so forth. They are particularly interested in certain aspects of systemic training, and they are going to use what they acquire throughout their training in different ways. For example, one intends to be taught systemic family therapy and afterwards to "transplant" the model of our family therapy clinic in the mental health facility to which the trainee belongs; another, who already practises some kind of psychotherapy, wants to integrate systemic therapy within it; another, who, apart from being a mental health professional, has been charged with managerial duties, is interested in assimilating the systemic approach and utilizing it with larger systems. Can supervision be differentiated according to the supervisee's expectations, goals, and idiosyncrasy? Can it be more individualized than uniform, as far as the boundaries of the training course allow for it? This is a current field of experimentation for both supervisors, which seems fascinating but risky as well.

CHAPTER 6

Some reflections on process, relationship, and personal development in supervision

Jeff Faris

The term "supervision" is used to cover a broad range of activities, including quality assurance of practice, management of service delivery, and case supervision. The term "clinical supervision" is not that much more specific, as it may refer to case management where the supervisor has clinical responsibility. It could also refer to case consultation as part of a therapist's ongoing professional development, or it could refer to live supervision of clinical practice as part of clinical training. These activities are not mutually exclusive, and there is a degree of overlap between them. It may be useful to distinguish between these activities, and in this chapter I refer mainly to "supervision" within the context of teaching systemic psychotherapy.

In this chapter, personal development as an aspect of supervision in a psychotherapy training context is the focus for some personal reflections. What follows includes a personal narrative or a version of my own experience of supervision. As much for the sheer narcissistic pleasure of indulging in my own reflections, I have also maintained a personal view in keeping with a typical exercise that may be required of a trainee therapist. Such an exercise would invite a trainee to recall past experience of supervision and reflect upon how this experience influences his or her current perspectives as a practitioner in supervision. If an exercise is considered useful for trainees' experience, could not a similar exercise be of benefit to a supervisor? As I have a keen interest in getting to grips with process, which proves to be highly elusive, I thought it would be useful to write this chapter on process and supervision as a reflective narrative and find out what the experience would bring forth. I would also find out what I would be willing to record and what I would prefer to keep to myself. The relationship between the personal epistemology embodied in therapists' practice and the discourses of espoused theory about therapy seems central to this process (Schön, 1983).

This distinction between personal epistemology and espoused theory introduced by Lynn Hoffman at the 1998 Dartington Conference inspired a lively and useful debate on the relationship between theory and process. Personal epistemology I see as forming a history of a practitioner's experience, prior training experiences, personal life events and beliefs, preferred responses and habitual reactions—what practitioners do in their work with clients and learn from this activity. Espoused theory I see as the type of activity that takes place outside practice with clients and usually between professional colleagues. It is the learned activity of discourse within the professional forum. It may take the form of practitioners seeking to share their knowledge, whether this is within a team or at a professional conference. It may take the form of practitioners being asked to justify their approach to fund holders or to service management audits. A typical gender stereotype would be that the discourse between male practitioners tends to be task-driven whereas that between female practitioners tends to be organized around relationship-building. The interface between theories and the shared understanding of theory applied to practice between supervisor and trainee is pertinent to the supervisory relationship. My own view is that ideas always have a life through relationships.

How ideas are presented to trainees as part of clinical supervised training will have a crucial influence on what they will learn and experience. I find that the most interesting and intangible aspect of supervision is the changing quality of relationship in the process of forming an interactional system of the supervisor, trainees, and clients (whether the clients are actually present or in the thoughts of the team and supervisor). It seems to me that the vast body of psychotherapy literature is to some extent a great enterprise attempting to find a language of process, each approach using its preferred metaphors to do so. Jonathan Potter (1993) holds the view that psychology as a discipline has not adequately addressed process. I wish to elaborate briefly on two complementary approaches to thinking and consider some implications of these operating within wider systems before focusing on the relationship between supervisor and practitioner in a training context.

Process, text, and relationship

In my opinion, most urban industrial technologically sophisticated culture does not successfully get to grips with any discourse of process. Within literary cultures (as opposed to oral traditions), technical literature and textbooks seek for the most part to define terms as clearly and as specifically as possible, aiming for accuracy of definition and avoidance of ambiguity.

Most discourse is driven by an imperative to define some "thing" as precisely as possible in order for it to be classifiable, have specific meaning, and be universally identifiable with precision. In contrast, by way of example, written Chinese has been described by the Sinologist Allan Watts as non-linear ideographic. Each ideogram conveys at once a concept and a complex constellation of relationships or gestalten that would require long, strung-out alphabetical sentences in a linear phonetic script (Watts, 1975). Kee Jin (personal communication 2000), a Tai Chi Chuan practitioner and a teacher and scholar of Tai Chi and Taoist classical texts, confirms this view from his perspective of familiarity with both Chinese and English translations. This view is also elaborated upon by Eward De Bono in his book, *Water Logic* (1993). He defines "rock logic" as a way of defining the world by classification of how something ostensibly is in terms of its fixed position or characteristics. "Water logic" has a quality of flow and of leading towards. He tells the story of a young boy in Australia whose peers conspired to offer him the choice of two coins, a one-dollar coin and a two-dollar coin, the latter of which is smaller in size.

The boy chose the larger coin, to the amusement of his companions, who were aware of this larger coin's lesser monetary value. This trick was performed on him frequently by his peers until someone taking pity on the boy took him aside and pointed out to him that the smaller coin was worth more money. The boy said he had already realized this but, had he chosen the two-dollar coin in the first place, he would have ceased to be the recipient of so many one-dollar coins.

Much of my clinical psychology training in Pretoria in the late 1970s veered sharply between these two perspectives. On the one hand there was an emphasis on diagnostic assessment rooted in classification of pathology, on the other a passionate zeal among many of my supervisors for phenomenological and constructivist approaches rooted within a humanistic tradition of psychotherapy. All of this took place within the context of the neocolonial former regime of South Africa.

My personal world-views, however, were predominantly rooted in Buddhist and Taoist orientations. From these perspectives it was easy for me to take the leap into systemic thinking, in all its permutations available to me at the time. Systems thinking I believed to be a recognized tradition of scientific enquiry within diverse fields. I believed that systems concepts afforded me a language to communicate ideas that I failed to translate from their Buddhist or Taoist traditions. I kept the Buddhist and Taoist views very much to myself. (As a South African of Lebanese Byzantine Catholic cultural background and Anglo/Teutonic descent, things were complicated enough.)

Early influences

My introduction to systems approaches began with my clinical psychology internship (full-time clinical-practice placement) at a psychiatric hospital in South Africa. Colleagues who were students from a neighbouring university were on fire with enthusiasm for interactional approaches strongly influenced by the Mental Research Institute model.

Having formed an unofficial network of peer supervision, we began to consult to one another. This was an invaluable experience, and peer-supervision-directed learning still forms an essential part of the psychotherapy training at the Family Institute in Cardiff as well as at many other training courses in the field. (With this, the virtue of the "unofficial" aspect may, unfortunately, be lost.) After several months of problem-based learning, I felt, however, that I was reaching an impasse with certain cases. Following enquiries through colleagues at this neighbouring university for some supervision of my work, I was offered the opportunity to meet regularly with Stan Lifschitz. Stan, together with another colleague, David Fourie, had been developing Ericksonian approaches to brief therapy at the University of South Africa and in their private practice. While their practice was focused on hypnosis and the work of Milton Erickson, their epistemology, however, was rooted in a systemic approach (Fourie, 1991).

My meetings with Stan were extremely challenging while simultaneously validating and encouraging. The challenge for me was to keep up with his invitations to leap self-imposed conceptual constraints. Each meeting seemed to pose a form of the nine-dot problem (Watzlawick, Weakland, & Fisch, 1974). Each time I found a way around this, I was invited to reflect on how I was doing this. The case supervision and discussion of papers he suggested were isomorphic with the model. The content of the papers and book chapters were one thing: the discussion of these papers itself was always an invitation to engage with the supervisory relationship. Whatever the content of the issues I would bring to supervision, Stan would respond either directly or indirectly at a relational level.

There was always space to talk about current and past personal transitions, struggles, and aspirations. There was openness to reflection on the supervisory relationship and an invitation to metacommunicate. I did not always choose to metacommunicate, as some things were best left as metaphor. Unpacking the story or analogy would demean or de-mean the point taken. Stan's responses to how I was—to what I showed or brought of myself—could at times be very direct and surprising and could cut through my confusion. I learned at first hand about compassion in both its gentle and its wrathful forms.

The contract with Stan was for supervision of cases and skills development. It was not for personal therapy. The experience was, however, profoundly therapeutic and had a significant impact on my personal development.

Personal development, training, and supervision

I once was told about a champion tennis coach who said that everyone potentially is able to be a competent tennis player, up till the time they meet a tennis coach.

His approach was strongly influenced, I guess, by his experience and view of coaches. He invited would-be tennis players to look at a tennis ball and notice the pattern on the ball. He would then suggest that one could notice the shadow on one side of the ball and the other hemisphere of the ball illuminated by the sun. He said that one could hit the ball through the air and practise doing this until one could observe the light and shaded areas of the ball in flight. When players were able to achieve this, they would find that they were hitting the ball at just the right height to clear the net. Instructing people to clear the net invariably resulted in them hitting the net. He did not use standard methods of teaching but tailored tasks and exercises to the style and temperament of each player. This principle has been refined to an art form in the work of Milton Erickson. It also is well established as an ideal among many supervisors on clinical training programmes with whom I have talked over the years.

Looking back over my own experience as a supervisor, this ideal has not been realized as often as I would wish. There have been times when I know I lost this perspective and became overly preoccupied with the objectified baseline criteria of formal assessment. At these times, it was easy, due to my preoccupation, to miss opportunities for creativity in facilitating or recognizing a trainee's accomplishment.

By way of illustration, I once heard of a primary-school teacher who asked the class to identify animals on a chart hanging in the classroom. The teacher, pointing at the sheep, asked Ailish. She looked hesitant and began to say, "I don't know . . .". To save Ailish any further embarrassment, the teacher immediately asked Johnny, who confidently replied: " It's a sheep!" Satisfied with the answer, the teacher never got to hear the end of Ailish's sentence, which would have been, ". . . whether it is a Merino or an Angora."

Presuppositions about adequate trainee response, status within the supervisory group, relationship to learning in an adult context, individual styles of learning, and gendered patterns of discourse are some of the factors affecting judgement of performance. The supervisor's sense of self in his or her role as teacher is also a powerful factor. How the supervisor balances baseline criteria of assessment and his or her aesthetic clinical sense may also be affected by external factors—for example, during periods of external scrutiny of the organization and of its training. Methods of validation, methods of audit, and methods of assessment in training both challenge and stimulate creativity in systemic thinking and practice. Opportunity for reflection on the impact of these processes, however, is also extremely useful.

In my view, an understanding of the self of the trainee therapist is intrinsically connected to the supervisor's understanding of her/himself within the supervisory relationship. This must be seen, too, in the light of what else is going on for them in their life (past, present, and future).

Space in this chapter does not allow scope to do justice to the wide field of enquiry into the nature of self and identity. The social constructionist concept of a self that is continuously being self-generated, is interactionally defined, and can change significantly has been elaborated and critiqued by various writers (e.g. Andersen, 1990; Anderson & Goolishian, 1988; Coupland & Nussbaum, 1993; Flaskas, 1999; Gergen, 1991; Goffman, 1961; Jones, 1993). Recently, too, predominantly Eurocentric perspectives within the field of family therapy have begun to be enriched by views from a wider and more global range of human experience (e.g. Association for Family Therapy, 2000; Flemons, 1991) I would like therefore to join with this wider perspective and contribute a view within a Buddhist view, which also has a long tradition of addressing questions of suffering, compassion, and human identity.

Chogyam Ogyen Rinpoche, in a public talk given in Cardiff in 1999, discussing referentiality as a process of defining self and identity, cited Descartes's well-known statement: "I think, therefore I am." This statement derives from Descartes's search for certain knowledge. This search led him to the one thing he could be in no doubt about—namely, his own state of doubting. The Buddhist version of Descartes' pronouncement would be: "I don't think, therefore what?"

Chan Buddhist and Tibetan Tantric Buddhist views would invite us to consider the possibility that we are continuously recreating our reality instant by instant. Stilling the mind sufficiently in order to perceive the gap between one instant and the next and then making the gap wider would reveal to us the matrix of our being. Though unqualified to hold forth on this experience, I am, however, inspired to consider in what ways I cling onto particular reference points in order to construct a particular version of my identity within a given context. I am also interested in how participants in a supervision group construe their sense of self in the process of their training and, in particular, how they reflect upon this process within the structured components of the supervised training focusing specifically on personal development. In order to make this connection more apparent, I need first to elaborate further the Buddhist views previously mentioned. I shall refer to the Tibetan Tantric practice of Trek Chod and emotional experience, with particular attention to the experience of intense emotions.

With regard to this view that we are continuously engaged in a process of defining ourselves through referential constructions of ourselves, Chogyam Rinpoche invited us to examine our referential notions of ourselves by using the Cartesian dictum and substituting any number of words instead of the word "think". What might we become aware of in relation to how we define our selves?

"I am a helpful therapist, therefore I am."
"I suffer, therefore I am."
"I am respected by my trainees, therefore I am."
"I don't know who I am, therefore I am."
"I am married to Prof. So-and-so, therefore I am."

Although there may be identifiable themes or life-scripts that we could describe, no single reference point completely defines who we are. We comprise a constellation of reference points.

By introducing the dimension of time into this equation, we can perhaps distinguish different constellations of self or personhood that take on different characteristics depending on our angle of perception and also depending on the time frame of our observation.

Tom Paterson (1996) distinguishes two perspectives on self in systemic theory: "relational self" and "autonomous self". He defines the relational self as initiating and accommodating in interaction with all the elements in the system. The relational self may or may not stay the same. He sees the autonomous self as having a structure formed by prior relational experience. The "autonomous self", if my reading of Paterson is correct, emerges as having continuity when considered or observed over time. The "relational self", therefore, would represent a cross-sectional aspect of self which nonetheless could influence the "autonomous self" depending on the thresholds of difference encountered by the "autonomous self" within this relational world. Paterson maintains that people do not continuously learn but may do so when meeting new circumstances.

The Buddhist practice of Trek Chod, however, involves a practice of cessation of referential concepts in relation to intense emotion. Total immersion and identification with the emotion without the usual accompanying referential sub-vocal dialogue—for example, "I am angry because . . . and therefore I exist"—results in the transformation of the emotion by itself .

This practice is based on the view not that as sentient beings we are gradually evolving towards an enlightened state (Tibetan: *Rigpa*), but that we are all already enlightened now and are working frantically to convince ourselves that we are not. This creates or brings forth the experience of being substantial, permanent, separate, continuous, and defined—that is, a dualistic view of experience. According to the view that we are convincing ourselves that we are not enlightened and that all of our moment-to-moment experiences are reflections (all be it distorted reflections) of our original Enlightened nature, every sentient experience is therefore an opportunity for transformation. Dualistic perceptions of emotions into positive and negative do not grasp the essential complementarity of these apparently dual polarities.

Transformation of dualistic polarities

What follows is a précis of the practice of Trek Chod outlined in greater detail by Chogyam Ngakpa and Khandro Dechen (1997).

Distracted from our enlightened original nature, we perceive it as threatening to our dualistic view that we are permanent, continuous, separate, defined, and substantial. Each of these qualities has a complementary reflection of Enlightenment. (As Enlightenment transcends qualification, these qualities are described as reflections of Enlightenment.) Taking each of these in turn, Buddhist teachings on the psychology of self consider how we convince ourselves that we are not Enlightened:

- In the face of our Enlightenment, as it begins to sparkle through the distractions we conjure, we experience impermanence of the world we construct. Preciousness over one's sense of pride or territory is a reaction to our insecurity. It is a distorted perception of no-thing-ness. Once we realize the security of no security then clinging to territory transforms into the experience of being centred.
- Along similar lines, perception of our Enlightened state is mistaken for a threat to our sense of permanence. This evokes anger and the impulse to destroy the threat. Anger transforms into clarity, its complementary reflection of Enlightenment.
- Our sense of separateness from original Enlightened nature is mistaken for isolation, which in turn evokes the desire to consummate with someone or something that will make us feel complete and not so alone. This transforms into compassion.
- The threat to our sense of definition evokes groundless anxiety or paranoia. This transforms into appropriate action in the face of whatever arises.
- The vastness of our original nature arises as emptiness, depression, or despair, which transforms into the wisdom of openness.

Recognizing that all these dualistic experiences are reflections of Enlightenment, the practice of Trek Chod, therefore, recognizes all experiences as opportunities for transformation. The cessation of referential thinking allows the experience to transform or relax into its original nature, the Buddhist question here being "I don't think, therefore what?" as opposed to "I think, therefore I am." How does one, then, as a being distracted from one's immanent Enlightenment, utilize everyday experience as an opportunity for such transformation? How does one deal with the range of intense and often negative emotional reactions to what everyday life throws up?

Intense emotion as opportunity for transformation

Paradoxically, total and exaggerated immersion in the negative intense emotional reaction without the usual accompanying referential sub-vocal dialogue "I am . . . and therefore I exist" results in the transformation of this emotional experience into its complementary reflection of Enlightenment. This can be explored through personal empirical experimentation using the method outlined below.

Personal empirical experimentation requires the ability to become aware of an intense emotional reaction as it arises. There is therefore a gap (Tibetan: *Bardo*) between the emotional reaction and the reflection on this fact.

Acting within the gap between the intense emotional reaction and one's awareness of its arising, one immerses oneself totally in the feeling. Where is the feeling located in one's body? This is not an experience of observing the emotional feeling but of dissolving all referential frames of identity. One does not think about the emotion, but becomes completely identified with it. Subject and object dissolve.

The presence of pure awareness arises, and of itself the negative emotion transforms into its positive complement.

While there is still a dualistic perception, there will be a gap between subject and object, this and that, cause and effect, and so forth following multiple distinctions and frames of reference which bring forth the configuration of experience and identity.

From the perspective of these Tibetan teachings within the Nyingma tradition of Tantric Buddhism, Enlightened beings are those who are no longer distracted by dualistic experience and therefore are no longer engaging in a frantic effort to convince themselves that they are not Enlightened, that they are not conditioned by what arises within the sphere of experience. Their actions arise spontaneously and unconditioned.

There is no manipulation here, no attempt to practise this exercise in order to change the arising emotion into something else that you think is better in terms of whatever referential framework you are operating. The transformation can only occur of itself when you (or your particular preferred version of you) disappear.

What, then, are the many marvellous and terrible ways in which we obscure our potential? Having outlined this spectrum of emotional possibilities, how, then, might one utilize this exercise? An example of this in the context of personal development within psychotherapy training at the Family Institute in Cardiff will hopefully address to some extent the second of these questions. I need first to describe briefly the nature of the experiential group and locate this aspect of the training within the context of personal development on the course.

What frames of reference, therefore, might be useful in considering the nature of selfhood within systemic supervision? This question has been considered for some time within the context of training at the Family Institute and with specific reference to meeting requirements of the U.K. Council for Psychotherapy that accredited training courses in psychotherapy must address the personal development of the trainee therapist. This applies also to supervision as a component of the continuing professional development of the qualified therapist. What follows is an overview of how my colleagues and I have sought to address this aspect of supervision in a training context. I then give a very brief outline, with examples, of how I have approached this task within the experiential group.

Clinical supervision and personal development of qualifying-level trainees at the Family Institute, Cardiff

Personal development is an integral aspect of the clinical supervision on the clinical training programme. Therapist use of self in live clinical supervision and video review, trainees' portfolios logging personal development, regular one-to-one meetings with supervisors and peer supervision provide a focus for context-related personal development. In addition, the trainees participate in a series of ninety-minute group meetings (60 hours in total) focusing on personal development.

The approach to this personal-development group has taken a variety of shapes over several years. In prior years this group was externally facilitated to explore the impact of training on the interface between trainees' personal, professional, and family life; this was a non-assessed course requirement. Currently, all formal aspects of personal development are facilitated by the teaching staff. This has been in response to feedback from former trainees and former external group facilitators. The trainees often felt that they preferred to address aspects of self in supervision groups with their supervisor and supervision-group members.

We decided to retain the personal-development group, but to structure it to comprise three sequential blocks each facilitated by a different member of staff and repeated in each of the two years of the qualifying-level course. There are three facets reflectively linked within each of these sequential blocks: self-reflection, academic group-work, and experiential group-work.

The following areas are explored in the light of the above:

1. Impact of the course on the life of the trainees.
2. Explorations of the nature of self and different beliefs held within the group on this. For example, self as creative process/ narrative versus self as structure.
3. Awareness of self in interaction with others, including group-member reflection on interactional processes within the training group.
4. Exploration of the relationship between self and others in the context of race, class, culture, and gender, including experience of diversity, difference, and discrimination.
5. Narratives across generations within families, pertinent to the development of a professional therapeutic identity.
6. Narratives across generations of psychotherapy and other professional training that have influenced trainees' views of themselves.

Each block in the cycle has a specific focus or theme. My role is to facilitate the experiential approach to personal development in the first block of the three-block cycle. The second block, facilitated by Ros Draper, tracks the history of concepts of self. The third block focuses specifically on the self in the context of culture, race, and gender and is facilitated by Brenda Cox.

Locating each block at two points in the course, approximately a year apart, allows perception of difference over time. Trainees would have experience of different facilitators each addressing different dimensions of personal development and each doing so via different modalities (didactic, experiential, anecdotal). The trainee group would remain constant. Each block would set something going and then allow this to develop independently of the facilitator while the group formed a different link with the next block. Each facilitator would then reconnect with the trainee group at a different point in their development over the two-year period of live supervised practice.

Some aspects of the first block, the experiential group, are now highlighted. Note that, in practice, each of the three blocks has incorporated a significant experiential dimension.

Experiential group

The orientation upon which I have based the experiential group has been generally outlined in the foregoing discussion in this chapter. The thinking behind running this group, discussed with the trainees at the outset, has been to provide a space in which to explore the way each person selects frames of reference in the process of negotiating certain aspects of human interactional systems:

Any human interactional system in formation will include the questions:

- "How does this group of individuals come to be interacting with one another in this situation at this time?"
- "How is inclusion and exclusion decided?"

- "What degree of intimacy or distance will occur?"
- "How will power and control be decided and by whom?"

These questions are by no means mutually exclusive and are not usually explicitly stated, but they may be understood implicitly by prior social or cultural cues or context markers (Faris, 1997, p. 3).

Trainees were invited as a group to notice what it was that provided the content of this negotiation. They were invited individually to notice what formed a focus of their awareness, how they did this, and how their awareness changed.

If one cannot not communicate (Haley, 1963; Watzlawick et al., 1967), by the same token one cannot not offer a definition of relationship and thereby a definition of self. Focusing on their here-and–now experience of the edges between individual agency, personal responsibility, and group cohesion, trainees were invited to try out different possible selves for size, with the understanding that these could always be put back on the shelf.

Fundamental to the initial stages was attention to group process, boundaries of confidentiality, perceptions of safety, negotiation of personal and group goals, and setting a context for serious play (Thompson Drewal, 1992).

My role as facilitator in the group was participative while holding a mandate from the other participants to track and monitor group process. Questions raised by myself or others or anecdotes told would often be in response to perceptions of relational patterns or shifting definitions of relationship between group members. I sought to cultivate awareness of the intent of my actions, questions, responses, anecdotes, comments, and so forth but did not seek to determine outcomes. The respective merits and deficits of direct or indirect communication were discussed by the group. When is it useful to metacommunicate and when is it counterproductive? In response to some of these questions or analogies, group members would initiate highly creative interactive games and exercises.

To re-present here in this text some of these experiential interactions out of their actual relational, temporal, and physical context is impossible. Two exercises, however, are described by way of illustration.

An exercise in metacommunication

An exercise devised by Barry Mason (1994) was adapted to the training context. The trainees are invited to write their names on a piece of paper and place these in a "hat", from which each trainee pulls out one name (not his or her own). The group are then invited to engage in a discussion, with each person doing so in the style of the person whose name they have drawn. At the end of a twenty-minute period, the facilitator engages in discussion to establish which aspects of personal style could be recognized and to whom they were attributed.

In this discussion, in which the participants reflect upon the experience of the exercise, how the facilitator uses circular questioning to open up an exploration of perceptions of self is crucial. The process of this discussion is central to the establishment of a context for giving and receiving feedback in a manner that is challenging enough to feel safe and playful enough to be taken seriously. Group members would, of necessity, have already had opportunity to establish sufficient familiarity with one another to engage meaningfully in this exercise.

Building upon this exercise, how, then, could participants be invited to view their own experience of themselves and one another with compassion and embrace common themes of human resourcefulness and stuckness, suffering and euphoria, wisdom and folly?

An exercise on cultivating compassion for oneself and for one's intense feelings.

Not underestimating the possible impact of supervision within a psychotherapy training, I wondered whether an exploration of self and identity inspired by the Tibetan practice of Trek Chod might be of benefit. As I write this chapter and reflect on what I have written, the differences between post-hoc description and the activity of engaging in the experiential exercises becomes increasingly stark.

The distinction made between personal epistemology and espoused theory earlier in this chapter comes into focus. During the experiential block, I did not expound upon Trek Chod and Tibetan

Tantra as I have felt it necessary to do here in a chapter of a book. What I brought to the group was more a personal epistemology and less espoused theory. I made reference to Tibetan Tantra or Vajrayana Buddhism by way of citing sources, but focused on inviting participants to follow and initiate a series of experiences and then reflect upon these.

In this chapter, which is a reflection on process, the thinking behind my thinking seems more apt. What would complement this account and complete the picture would be for the trainee group to read what I have written and write their own responses. (Although feedback from trainees is in progress, it is not sufficiently advanced for inclusion in this text.)

Within the experiential group, however, because the process of dialogue and the ability to respond to feedback and thereby discover new directions was possible within the group, it did not seem to me to be useful nor necessary to elaborate the thinking behind my thinking to the group members as I have done here. This could be addressed by questions from the group and a collective awareness of where the energy of the group was going. It seemed to me to be better just to get on with it.

What I did was to invite the group members to engage in an exercise in awareness. (This was one area that many group members had said they wished to explore.) Could they become aware of what they noticed from moment to moment, here and now, in the room? Would this include thoughts about events outside the present such as past and future recollections or preoccupations? What was their awareness of the quality of their experience emotionally? Boredom? Indifference? Heightened awareness? Self-consciousness? Curiosity? Inner calm? Anxiety? Impatience? Physical sensations? I did not offer these possibilities but wondered what my own and other group members' experiences would be.

Following this exercise was an exercise in having no thoughts at all—"I don't think therefore what?" Then, having had a go at this, I introduced an exercise in at least halting the inner sub-vocal dialogue. One could become aware of one's incoming and outgoing breath, just bringing awareness to this naturally without interfering with the way it is however it is. Our breath is right on the edge between voluntary and autonomic experience. We can control our breathing, and we can forget about it and it takes care of itself. The trainees were invited to allow sub-vocal thoughts or commentary to do what they liked on one breath (inspiration or expiration), and on the next breath to see if they could just be aware without sub-vocal commentary. This could be just (but not merely!) sensory awareness.

Following a discussion on each one's experience, I was also aware of how each person responded to the exercise and how each one offered a definition of her/himself in doing so within the context of the group and against the background of the group's shared history. I was aware that my observation, opinion, and judgement of knowing how to go on would be influenced by the structure of the overall theme I was building within these tasks, alongside the responsiveness of each group member to me and to each other.

Having invited the group members to explore an aspect of their own event (being), we then engaged in a discussion about how we construe ourselves in relation to our perception of the boundaries between self and other. How do we draw distinctions from moment to moment between the various frames of reference and thereby define ourselves? The role of emotions, in particular powerful and overwhelming emotions, had previously emerged as a theme for discussion and was once again brought into focus.

The trainees were therefore then invited specifically to consider a recollection of an experience in the context of their practice when they experienced intense emotion. This was something that each could recall, initially silently on their own. After a while, I asked the group to consider how their experience might fit with the following:

> "When beleaguered by organizational, interpersonal, accidental, and inevitable stress or affronts to one's sense of identity what resources are available to one?"

I suggested a number of ways in which one could, as a therapist, focus on one's own "internal" experience of self. (This exercise could just as well serve for supervisors in reflecting upon their supervision practice. The version here, however, is the one used in the personal-development group.)

1. When one finds oneself in a therapy session being knocked off balance, or feeling that one's "territory" is being eroded, then become territorial or try frantically to regain balance at all costs even though this, metaphorically speaking, leaves one with arms flailing about desperately in the attempt. Probably the best way to regain balance may be to let go of the attempt to hold it or reclaim it. What would they try?

2. When one finds one's concept of self threatened by challenge (whether the challenge is reasonable or totally unjust), then allow the fear to manifest as anger with the client, colleagues, supervisor, or oneself. As an alternative, deal with the threat by being appreciative of the opportunity to see things in a fresh way with new clarity and to let go of the image one is attempting to protect. What was being defended?

3. When one finds oneself erotically or otherwise attracted to a client, colleague, or supervisor, then indulge in this, or repress it, or berate oneself with shame; alternatively, develop an aversion towards this person. (For supervisors: If in the course of individual or group supervision one hears the therapist mention, hint, or vaguely allude to the possibility that he or she may be experiencing such feelings, immediately change the subject to the weather or to another case.) Alternatively one could acknowledge this experience and find ways to allow the passion to transform into compassion. Which experience would they recall, and could they be responsibly compassionate towards themselves?

4. When one finds oneself in a state of free-floating anxiety instead of focusing on what one perceives to be actually in the here-and-now, then one could become suspicious and paranoid in a vain attempt to nail down what it is. The alternative might be to embrace uncertainty and the possibility of being a little bit out of control in the event that something new and possibly exciting might come of it. What might they experience next?

5. When one feels a sense of hopelessness or impotence, then despair or try immediately to fill the gap instead of accepting one's sense of emptiness or accept that there will be empty

spaces where nothing seems to be happening or making any sense.

The trainees were invited to talk about the experience of reflecting in this exercise and they did not have to disclose any content they did not wish to discuss. Clearly, a large factor in facilitating this process was monitoring the balance of closeness or distance, intimacy or generality of experience within the group. What seemed to me to be most significant was that the following time the group met, some of them reported that the exercise had had an effect on their awareness of everyday experience as well as their professional work.

Dilemmas of addressing differences in how much individuals did or did not talk within the group was something to which I have given considerable thought. I have heard Tom Andersen on several visits to our team over the years stating that he respects the value both of talking and of listening. While I found that the group was generally well balanced in this respect, I did find myself on one occasion when the group seemed particularly pensive making reference to Tom Andersen's position on this and then asking the group what they thought. There was a moment of frozen silence, followed by howls of laughter and a useful discussion on what might contribute to processes of being relatively silent in the group or relatively active. Did individuals find themselves becoming defined by positions they may have taken at some point? What repeating patterns did they notice? What agency did they have in the status quo? What would they wish to keep the same, and what would they wish to change?

One systemic approach to supervision would regard any emotional experience of the therapist as valuable information about how the therapeutic system is organized. This information would be utilized by the therapist/supervisor repositioning her/himself vis-à-vis her or his own presuppositions and behaviour (Cecchin, 1987; Cecchin, Lane, & Ray, 1994). This is a compassionate and useful stance for the therapist to take in order to free her/himself to change. It is also a useful position for the supervisor to take within the supervision group. This allows the possibility for a contextual and interactional view that facilitates a rich exchange and pragmatic rather than judgemental responses.

Conclusions and further personal reflections on supervision groups and the training experience

Following my interest in the relationship between the personal epistemology embodied in therapists' practice and the discourses of theory about therapy, I have presented some personal views on supervision.

The background of the experiences I have described in this chapter leads me on to some reflections on personal development and the role of personal therapy in supervision and training.

In the light of the necessity and inevitability of discourses of professionalization, evidence-based practice, government initiatives on quality assurance of training courses, and occupational standards for psychotherapy and supervision, I often need to highlight for myself the personhood of trainees, ourselves as teachers and supervisors, and our relationship to these large-system discourses.

Bearing in mind the analogies of the Socratic tennis coach and the Tantric teachings of Tibetan Buddhism, I tell myself that all trainees or therapists seeking supervision are highly competent, expert therapists. At times they may work very hard to convince themselves and me that they are not. This in no way reflects on the way that any trainees or therapists I have met have engaged with the training or supervision process. This is entirely an intervention to myself lest I become stuck in my perception of "correct therapy" or "correct supervision". This, I hope, will enable me to remain curious as to how and what a trainee or therapist might be doing to obscure her or his natural, inherent therapeutic resourcefulness. My task then is not to add something, but to facilitate the removal of obstacles and the opening up of possibilities to the best of my ability.

A starting point that I have currently found to be useful in supervision is that of compassionate acceptance of one's own experience of what is. The term "acceptance" does not imply a passive acquiescence, but a robust, open, and curious embracing of what appears. I have not framed this as acceptance of another, but, rather, as an acceptance of one's own experience of another as the starting point. Without this awareness and acceptance of one's own responses, I do not believe that there can be any genuine acceptance of another person, nor any acceptance of responsibility. Transformation may only be possible from this position. This may be analogous with the Milan systemic view of how change is more likely under a positive connotation. What however of acceptance of what is not?

Comments

The chapters in this part have demonstrated how much training depends on the integration of theory, practice, research, and personal development. This integration can be supported by the structures and philosophy of training based on systemic principles. Included in this integration is the emphasis placed on a reciprocal relationship between trainers and trainees. This part has offered specific examples of ways trainees can give feedback that informs trainers about their style and shapes the structure of the training itself.

It is also interesting that the hierarchical aspect of supervision has been addressed by several "role reversals" whereby trainees interview trainers about their supervision, or trainees act as "live" supervisors of their own colleagues. What comes across to us is the way training maintains differences within the system—that is, hierarchical positions—and exploits these to generate feedback and broaden our understanding of what a "training system" really is.

There have been clear discussions in this part about the learning process. Responsibility for learning has emerged as a two-sided process that can be negotiated by both members of the supervisory relationship. Supervision draws on our personal, autonomous selves as well as our relational, or systemic, selves and we need to find ways to use both perspectives. Chapter six brought self-reflexivity into the spotlight but defined it as something required of both trainer and trainee for supervision to be effective. Doubts and dilemmas and personal or even physical responses can be addressed in supervision by both supervisor and supervisee staying close to the experience sufficiently until resolution begins to happen.

PART III

PERSPECTIVES ON PRACTICE

CHAPTER 7

Family therapy supervision in the context of an inpatient child and adolescent eating-disorders unit

Vivienne Gross

A systemic approach to supervision in the context of an inpatient treatment service for children and young people with serious eating disorders poses special and specific challenges.

This chapter describes one evolving example of trying to integrate the best of family therapy methods, supervisory systems, teamwork techniques, and psychological-medicine knowledge in addressing the complex difficulties that this client group and their families face.

Clinical vignettes are used to illustrate the ways in which the ideas are put into practice.

The author's approach to systemic supervision

The author-supervisor has extensive experience of supervisory work both within multidisciplinary health and social services settings (mostly child guidance/child and family consultation service settings) and within family therapy training institutions. These experiences include using a variety of supervisory methods, from reported discussion of families to live supervision and videotaped retrospective supervision.

The field of systemic supervision has developed alongside that of family therapy and systemic practice into mutually influencing reflexive patterns. Trailblazing practitioners such as John Byng-Hall and Rosemary Whiffen helped import supervisory methods that they had observed and learned either through visits to the United States or through workshops and conferences in this country to which overseas colleagues were invited. The ideas and techniques, of course, were adapted and made increasingly culturally coherent with the British field of family therapy and developed with their own British-context flavour (e.g. some of the more stylized use of self, the use of brash humour, and confrontational methods of unbalancing families were toned down and made more compatible, in cultural terms, with a British context).

The innovative potential of live supervision using a one-way screen and/or videotape facilities made a huge impact on the thinking about supervision in the early 1970s. For example, Byng-Hall and Whiffen (1982) focused on the supervisor's capacity to help supervisees move beyond "impasse" situations in therapy (Byng-Hall & Whiffen, 1982).

However, more recent perspectives on systemic supervision tend to take live supervision facilities for granted, focusing in far more depth and detail on the supervisor's relationship with the supervisee, as well as the supervisor's use of self in the supervision (see Burnham, 1993; Wilson, 1993).

My own preferred style of systemic supervision places an emphasis on:

1. *Creating a safe learning environment for the supervisee,* based on the importance of a secure supervisory base, within which the uncertainties of the supervisee can be held and managed in such a way that appropriate therapeutic risks can be taken (see Mason, 1993).

This base would usually be established via several team sessions involving team-building exercises, personal/professional work (such as looking at supervisees' own genograms in the group, "trigger" family issues, etc.), reading key papers together, and exchanging ideas on these, all prior to seeing a first family in the team context.

2. *Using the prior learning, skills, and knowledge-base of the supervisee as a resource* for elaborating and connecting to newly found and newly explored systemic methods and techniques. This includes having a conversation with the supervisee before each clinical session, in which the supervisee is placed as "central", and his or her hopes, fears, and preferences for how he or she should conduct the session and would like the supervision to be organized are elicited and given prominence. Questions to the supervisee would include a focus on the supervisee's beliefs about his or her professional strengths in his or her primary discipline, and the subsequent conversation would use the team, too, to help the supervisee develop his or her ideas about how these skills and advantages can be accessed and used in the family therapy context.
3. *Using a self-reflexive feedback model of teamwork,* in which the supervisee and team are asked to reflect after each session on how the session affected them, what they valued in their practice on that occasion, what they have learned via this particular session, and what they would like to do differently.

This part of the post-session feedback is kept, as far as is possible, separate from the team's and supervisor's feedback about family-focused issues, to which there is so often a magnet-like attraction.

By this I mean that most teams find it far easier and are more practised in talking about what they observe the family doing, how the family members are/are not changing, and so on . They tend to be far less easily drawn into thinking about and articulating how they saw the practitioner changing, or how they saw their own practice developing. My supervisory approach aims at a rigorous preservation of a significant part of the post-session time remaining dedicated to a supervisee/team focus, away from and distinct from any family focused talk.

4. *A preference for a collaborative, conversational approach* (as is clear from the foregoing description), very consistent with ap-

proaches to therapy itself as articulated by Gergen and Kaye (1992) as a "receptive mode of enquiry—with its openness to different ways of punctuating experience, readiness to explore multiple perspectives and endorse their coexistence . . ." (pp. 182–183).

The dilemmas of the blending of these preferred tenets of systemic supervision with the essentials of an inpatient treatment service in the context of a potentially life-threatening condition (anorexia nervosa) are explored further in the text.

The supervisory context

The author supervises in the context of a highly specialist hospital-based service, described below.

The inpatient Child and Adolescent Eating Disorders Unit is part of a newly established, comprehensive Child and Adolescent Eating Disorders Service (known as CAEDS), providing assessment, treatment, and follow-up for children and young people with a wide range of eating disorders—including the provision of outpatient, day-patient, and inpatient treatment programmes.

The age range is 7 to 17 years, with flexibility at the older age-range, and an important capacity for follow-through and transfer on to a long-established adult eating-disorders treatment service within the same hospital.

There are a number of associated research initiatives with strong links to the medical school of the same hospital group, which is on a nearby but separate site.

The unit is unique in the NHS in providing for this child and adolescent age-group an inpatient facility specializing exclusively in the treatment of eating disorders. Other comparable services provide outpatient-only facilities or accommodate the children and young people who are of most concern in inpatient beds that are part of broader-based adolescent psychiatric hospital wards.

The ethos of the service places family therapy as a central component of the overall treatment plan, with parental involvement in the recovery work being seen as crucial, along the lines of a two-stranded "partnership" model:

1. There is a need for the parents to establish a working partnership together in order to be able to manage their child's eating disorder effectively as a coherent working pair.
2. The treatment team needs to establish a close working partnership with the parents so as to work together successfully (professionals and family as a team) to support the child or young person to overcome his or her eating disorder.

The components of the treatment package

Refeeding. Most of the children and adolescents admitted to the unit will be emaciated on arrival. This has severe physical ramifications and needs to be addressed as both an immediate and a medium- to long-term problem.

To achieve refeeding, each child/young person will have a carefully tailored diet plan, individually discussed with her or him (by their key nurse) and overseen by a dietician. Mealtimes and snacktimes (three times and twice a day, respectively) are managed by nursing teams with additional multidisciplinary input. The nurses play a close supportive role with each of the children, encouraging them to eat and drink what is necessary for each of them according to their own diet plan, and helping them overcome fears of food and weight gain in as detailed a way as is often needed.

Although most of the children are anorexic, some are bulimic too, so mealtimes can also involve the nursing staff in providing vigilant support to the children to avoid and prevent binge-eating and/or vomiting, both of which interfere with healthy weight maintenance and physical well-being.

Milieu therapy. The nursing team and the multidisciplinary team provide a milieu in which the children and young people are encouraged to form relationships and interact with one another in a way that is both therapeutic and beneficial.

This involves mixing with other patients on the ward, relating with staff both in groups and in one-to-one sessions, and participating fully in the unit's programme of activities.

The overall aim of the milieu therapy is that the child/young person communicates well with staff and other patients (rather than becoming isolated or withdrawn), expresses anxieties, worries, and any other feelings in a way that deals with them and manages them, rather than focusing all negative emotions and anxieties into fears related to food, eating, and weight and body-shape.

Individual therapy. Each child/young person is offered weekly individual therapy sessions with a psychotherapist or counsellor. The aim of this is to provide an opportunity for individual, private reflection and exploration of difficulties that are created or maintained by the eating disorder.

Group therapy. All the children participate in a number of ward-based therapy groups addressing issues of self-esteem, assertiveness, body-communication skills, group processes on the ward, and many other topics, all of which play a part in facilitating recovery from the eating disorder. The groups are facilitated by members of the nursing team in collaboration with or under the supervision of various members of the multidisciplinary team.

Physiotherapy. Many of the children and young people have used excessive exercise as well as food restriction and/or vomiting to reduce their body weight to what are often dangerously low levels. This can result in withered muscles and thinning bones, leading to the risk of osteoporosis.

As a healthy and appropriate alternative to overly vigorous exercise, the children are included in appropriate levels of group stretching and muscle-toning under the supervision and guidance of a physiotherapist.

This facilitates a feeling of bodily well-being and fitness without further compromising their physical condition.

Music therapy. Many of the children and young people find verbal self-expression extremely difficult and "risky", but they can benefit greatly from the opportunity to explore difficult feelings and thoughts through musical expression in a safe, controlled, and therapeutic environment.

The children are provided with a range of musical instruments to try out and to use in harmony in coordination, or in contrast to the parallel playing of the music therapist, who helps them to make sense of and verbalize what they may have conveyed musically, at an appropriate time and pace, during the therapy sessions.

One-to-one sessions. Each of the children has a nursing "mini-team" consisting of first, second, and third key nurses, whom the children know have special responsibility for their care and continuing progress within the treatment programme.

They will have regular one-to-one sessions with these nurses to think through day-to-day difficulties and decisions, such as how to manage their eating when on home leave, relationships with other patients, potential changes to their diet plan (often a source of new anxiety), plans for a phased return home, school-based concerns, and so forth.

Family therapy. All children and young people in the unit are offered regular ongoing family sessions as part of the treatment package. Drawing on the findings of the Maudsley team (see Dare et al., 1995), family therapy, parental counselling, and parental involvement are seen as central elements in the effective and thorough recovery process for children and young people with eating disorders.

The principles underlying this part of the treatment package are that

- Family factors do *not* cause eating disorders.
- Eating disorders are often multi-causal, and only in very few cases are the causes ever identified.
- Families very readily feel *blamed* for not having prevented their child's illness—feelings of self-blame do not help parents to help their child recover from the eating disorder.
- Families benefit from significant available support to help

them to help their child face the ongoing fight against the illness.

- Family factors can inadvertently contribute to *maintaining* the illness, unless professional help is available to help work against that trend.
- Parental counselling can be an appropriate alternative to family therapy where (at any particular phase of the work) the clinical picture shows that work with child and family together is contraindicated.
- Family therapy is a key component in recovery for early-onset child and adolescent eating disorders.

Family sessions and parental counselling are crucial at the beginning of the child's stay in hospital, since the admission phase is often a crisis for the family—firstly in coming to terms with the seriousness of their child's condition, and secondly in separating from her or him at this crisis time.

Family sessions are also enormously important at later stages in treatment, when the child/young person begins to recover, becoming well enough for day, overnight, or weekend visits home to be planned. Typically, families have often become nervous about challenging their child's eating behaviour in the earlier stages of the illness, for fear of her or his reactions to imposed eating suggestions by parents.

Families benefit from talking through together, with professional support, how they can pull together to support their child's recovery and reintegration into family life and also plan how they can build into family life aspects of the unit's approach that help the young person to maintain and continue an appropriate weight gain.

Siblings in the family often have strong feelings about the child/young person with the eating disorder and may feel a mixture of enormous relief that their sibling is out of danger, alongside feelings of rivalry to the point of perhaps feeling neglected by parents who have been so caught up with the care of the "ill" sibling. Family sessions can provide an important neutral environment for addressing potentially explosive dynamics that could be experienced as too volatile to manage in the family's own home.

The organization of the family therapy service

The family therapy teams are organized as four half-day sessions, with the same supervisor (the author) in each, but with different team compositions. Families will see the same therapist with the same supervisor and (broadly) the same team for each appointment.

The teams meet and see families within the environment of the Prudence Skynner Family Therapy Clinic (PSFTC), using the clinic's operational policies and administrative systems.

The PSFTC provides a discrete therapy service (with its own head of discipline) and is part of the Psychotherapy Directorate, which is one of a range of services called Highly Specialist Services within the South West London and St. George's NHS Mental Health Trust.

The family therapist/supervisor for the CAEDS (the author) is employed by the PSFTC and seconded into the CAEDS for the majority of the working week.

The therapists for the families of the children and young people with eating disorders will be either the family therapist/supervisor (the author) or other members of the various dedicated family therapy teams, working under live supervision.

The teams are made from a multidisciplinary mix of nurses, clinical assistants, social workers, junior doctors, senior registrars, individual therapists, and occasional visiting doctors, therapists, researchers, or clinical psychologist.

The therapists for the families may have had the opportunity to learn about family systems theory by attending the foundation course in family therapy (based at the PSFTC) or they may have been exposed to systemic ideas in their core trainings (such as social work, psychology, or medicine).

Other therapists may be members of the nursing team who value family therapy experience both for the added interpersonal skills they may gain which will enhance wider aspects of their work within the ward context, as well as wanting the family therapy experience as part of a longer-term career plan.

The team-and-screen setting for the family sessions is routinely used, as are videotape facilities (where child and parents consent).

The use of reflecting teams is a valued tradition in the PSFTC and is often experienced as a less threatening way for the more inexperienced practitioners to become directly involved in family therapy sessions, without having prime responsibility for the conducting of the session(s).

Most families appreciate and warm to this approach, and it is used frequently but not exclusively. All supervisees have an appropriate length experience of participation in family therapy team-work (whether behind the screen or as a member of reflecting teams) prior to becoming the supervised therapist for one of the families.

Adapting the author's supervisory model to the CAEDS inpatient context

In any supervisory system, there are inherent contradictions and competing demands to which the supervisor will need to pay prior attention, with an appropriate balance achieved.

I characterize these issues as a series of priorities or responsibilities, which I organize as follows:

1. *Responsibility towards the clients, in an agency context*—that the quality of service must be assured. By this I mean that the highest "context marker" is that the child/young person and her or his family receives an adequately competent, skilled, and responsive family therapy service. (That is, in an agency context—where clinical services to families, training opportunities, research, income-generation, administration, liaison with other services, policy development, and other activities may all compete for professional priority—the context marks out that the highest-ranking activity is, in this example, the responsibility towards the clients for the service they receive.)

2. *Responsibility towards the supervisee*—that they experience an enabling, facilitative, safe, learning, and developmental practice opportunity from the supervisor and within the team environment.
3. *Responsibility towards the team members behind the screen*—that they experience an involving, validating, and learning-focused participation in the clinical work.

I see these three as hierarchically organized, so that (1) is always a priority over (2), and (1) and (2) are prioritized over (3) similarly. However, when ideal conditions apply, all three can be happening successfully simultaneously!

For example, where the therapist under supervision has reached a competent and confident level of practice and also has a good therapeutic link with the family they are seeing, and a smooth running pattern of communication exists between the therapist and the supervisor, the supervision of the therapist is mostly "contextual". That is, the pre-session discussion between the therapist, supervisor, and team provides the springboard for the session's beginning stage, and the easy flow of the process between the participants in front of the screen allows the supervisor to concentrate on "developmental" interventions for the supervisee, and freedom also to connect these exchanges to the evolving conversations between the supervisor and the other team members behind the screen (with a more training-oriented focus).These can then be synthesized into post-session hypothesizing and feedback discussions for both clinical and training uses.

Bringing my supervisory model to the CAEDS inpatient context has posed particular challenges, and the growing experience of the team-work involved in the inpatient part of the service and its "organic" relationship to the family therapy teams has given rise to very different perspectives on the optimal supervisory approaches in this context. The main issues that have emerged are:

- limitations of a collaborative approach
- neutrality
- boundaries

Limitations of a collaborative approach

When the clinical team of the CAEDS has an implicit responsibility to prevent a child/young person from dying, does the nature of a collaborative approach to family therapy become significantly compromised? That is, does anorexia nervosa in the frame drive out therapeutic creativity? Or does it perhaps push the pace of therapy differently from what would be the case were there a family presenting with, say, "relationship difficulties" or other more common but less medically/physically affecting family concerns?

> *Vignette 1*
>
> A common example of this would be where, for example, a supervisee is asking some questions of the family of an anorexic 14-year-old girl, Sarah, whose younger sister had died in the year before the onset of her illness, how they talk about difficult and sad issues in the family.
>
> [The supervisee is an experienced practitioner in his primary field, and this is his first session with his second family within the CAEDS context. The first family he worked with was extremely challenging and he found the family work very stressful. However, the child in that family had had a successful inpatient treatment and was discharged home after a long and useful series of family sessions, with ongoing planned outpatient support.]
>
> In this session the supervisee is respectfully and gingerly asking about communication patterns, how they had coped as a family with their traumatic bereavement, and he is receiving lots of "back-off" messages from the mother in reply, organizing the other family members to support the "no-difficult-talking" message.
>
> The supervisor is challenged by the dilemma of supervising the practitioner in a way that moves collaboratively at the pace of his development, taking firmly into account his feedback about how stressful he finds it to feel as though he is "pushing" families into painful areas of conversation.

On the other hand, the supervisor is also being affected by the belief that joining the family in a way that establishes that "difficult talk is outlawed here" may significantly delay the process of Sarah's recovery and may not help the family keep step with the support, encouragement, and rate of change (in fighting her anorexia nervosa) that Sarah is making on the ward.

Here is an example where clinical need (the family's receiving helpful enough therapy) jockeys for position with collaborative supervision methods, in the moment in which the supervisor's dilemma is sharply poised on issues of clinical judgement between supervisor and supervisee. To polarize it for simplicity:

Supervisee's position—"If I ask more about the bereavement, will I make things worse?"

Supervisor's position—"If he loses the opportunity to support the family in talking together about the death in the family, he may be caught up in maintaining family patterns that allow troublesome feelings in Sarah to be routed through her eating disorder, rather than processed in key relationships, perhaps contributing to the illness thriving for longer and/or becoming more entrenched."

In this example the supervisor was thinking about whether the urgency of the situation necessitated calling the therapist out of the room for a discussion encouraging him to be more forthright in pursuing "difficult talk" with the family, while reassuring him about his fears of pressing the family too far too fast, or whether to proceed in the usual way of the team and say something in the reflecting-team discussion that would touch on these issues (more indirectly than would be the case were the therapist to raise these topics in the face-to-face conversation with the family members themselves).

In this instance, the supervisor took the latter approach and broached the "difficult" topics in the reflecting-team discussion only, but she explored the dilemmas surrounding this choice with the therapist in the post-session discussion.

However, at a later stage in the girl's treatment, after a change of therapist (due to staff changes) the mother in the family confided that she preferred her new therapist's "straightforward no-nonsense" approach, perhaps feeding back that the initial therapist's sensitivity to the family feedback at the earlier point had been unhelpfully organizing him into rather too tentative an approach.

However, this family feedback was, of course, coming at a later stage of engagement with the CAEDS team in general, and the process of family therapy in particular, so this difference (in time) may need to be taken into account as playing a part in the mother's attitude to the therapists' perceived differences of style.

Neutrality

The family therapy teams are comprised of various groupings of colleagues from within the CAEDS. All these professionals are involved together in daily work with the children and young people on the ward and are a close-knit group of colleagues, with the concomitant intensity of staff dynamics ensuing that often results from the impact of inpatient work on staff teams.

One effect of this is that we are "passionate" about the families we see (both when behind as well as in front of the screen), because of the many-layered relationships we have with the children/young people. For example, a nurse colleague who in the morning is part of a reflecting team for a child and family may later on in the day be sitting with that same child at lunch, encouraging her to eat and reassuring her about her capacity to do so. Do these multiple roles, with differing levels of closeness and distance in different contexts compromise the meta-perspectives of the supervisor and of the other team members?

Over time, I am increasingly convinced that awareness of and vigilance over this issue within the team-working model allows us to challenge ourselves and each other when this passion may be becoming an unhelpful rather than a helpful team element.

The value of this quality of our work together is that the high degree of team commitment to the task, and to closely knit team-working practices, gives a strong sense of mutual support and "solidity" behind the therapist, enhancing the supervisory system and the commitment that each person appears to make to concentration and energetic rigour within the family therapy teams' thinking.

Boundaries

The different roles and responsibilities that the family therapy team members hold outside (i.e. in the CAEDS) have to be given careful attention in relation to how "special knowledges" held between the inpatient team and the family therapy team relate to one another.

The dilemmas arising here are hinged on the importance of binding the work of the supervisor and therapist effectively to the development and progress of the child/young person on the ward, and family therapy sessions are often especially aimed at helping the family stay connected and involved in that. On the other hand, responsive and sensitive family therapy practice has to follow the family's feedback too and explore issues and preoccupations that the family may have that do not necessarily appear to relate directly to the issues of fighting against and treating the eating disorder.

> *Vignette 2*
>
> For example, one single parent of a child, Sally, with anorexia was stressed and preoccupied with the difficulties she experienced in her relationship with her ex-husband's parents. She described feeling that these problems were becoming increasingly intrusive as a result of her daughter's serious illness and hospitalization (i.e. the child's grandparents expected more frequent telephone contact with the mother, to hear about Sally's progress and condition, so that the mother's previous pattern of distancing and keeping her parents-in-law at arm's length was proving harder to maintain in the new circumstances).
>
> These were the problems that Sally's mother wanted to talk about in the family sessions. However, the child's key nurse

> had come to the session hoping that Sally would be focusing with her mother on the new steps Sally was taking to follow all of her diet plan and her need for her mother to understand the special arrangements she would like to have for mealtimes at home, to enable her to have "home leave" without losing weight while away from the structured treatment and refeeding regime of the ward.
>
> The family therapy teams, with the supervisor's oversight, are constantly balancing the need to select and address the most important issue(s) in each session, where there are frequent differences between where the family's thoughts and preoccupations may lie and what the ward staff and the child are focused upon.

In this example, the therapist successfully talked through the mother's concerns, with Sally attentively involved too, so that some family solutions were arrived at, at least to think about and try in the future, without which the mother would not have been able to focus and think about Sally's next steps towards achieving a weekend at home. These were looked at towards the end of the session, with the mother by this stage feeling "heard" and her concerns understood.

Also, there may be complex difficulties where the child/young person or the parent(s) present material that they ask to be kept "confidential" from other parts of the CAEDS team or do *not* want discussed in family therapy, or where they ask that issues emerging in family therapy are not to be divulged during the ward round or to a key nurse, or to the consultant of the unit, or to some other specific professional.

The working model we have established is largely based on the principle that we are a multidisciplinary team, working together as a coherent treatment team, and that all parts of the service (including family therapy) are understood as contextualized by the overarching aim—that is, to provide effective, as short as possible, thorough treatment for the eating disorder. This leads to the tendency to see all material as potentially available to other professionals in the team, on a need-to-know basis, at the minimum sufficient level of detail.

At the start of the series of family sessions, all family members are told that the family meetings are a vital part of the child/young person's treatment package, and the emphasis is again placed on the "team approach", highlighting that all the family therapists and most of the team members behind the screen are part of the wider CAEDS and are therefore working to the same aims and priorities.

It is also stressed that although the family meetings are a time for more detailed, intimate discussions of child and family issues than is available in other ward-based meetings, there can be no "secrets" that are kept between the family and therapy team, away from the wider multidisciplinary team.

Similarly, the child and family are routinely made aware that the rigorous involvement of members of the ward nursing team as part of the family therapy team is a structural method that helps ensure that knowledge of the child/young person's dilemmas, difficulties, and progress on the ward does not become split-off and separate information—that is, hidden from view and kept away from the integration of its important meaning into the family sessions.

In discussing this with families, we also make it clear that key *themes* from family therapy sessions will be shared with colleagues (in the weekly ward round), but not specific details. On the other hand, the keeping of specific secret/private issues would be unlikely to be agreed to by any individual practitioner in the team, unless there were a very clear therapeutic/safety rationale for such an agreement to be made—for example, child-protection or domestic violence issues may need to be dealt with separately or confidentially within a specific professionally agreed strategy.

Vignette 3

An example of the dilemmas of "openness" and "privacy" is that of Ashleigh, who has been suffering from anorexia nervosa for two and a half years and has a previous history of successfully achieving weight gain back to a near-normal healthy level but, when her discharge planning becomes imminent, reverts to anorexic behaviour and rapidly reduces her weight again.

This prevents and delays plans for considering a return home to her family. Her twin brother and her older sister are desperate to help her and would like to understand more about her illness and how she might recover, but Ashleigh has said to her key nurse that she fears confiding in them because of their perceived closeness to her parents.

She has been admitted to the unit on this occasion with a strong commitment to getting well this time, saying she is fed up with her life in hospital and wants to live fully again. However, she finds it extraordinarily difficult to talk to her family about the dilemmas of returning home, and she has asked a nurse to tell the therapist about this so that she can feel safe in the family sessions.

The nurse passes on the information to the family therapist in a way that is coherent with the therapeutic alliance she has established and wishes to maintain with Ashleigh. However, the receiving of the information puts the family therapist in a position of having "privileged" information that the parents currently do not have access to, potentially binding her position much more closely to that of the young patient than to that of her parents.

The therapist arranges a three-way meeting with herself, the key nurse and Ashleigh in preparation for the next family session, so as to have an exchange in which Ashleigh can voice her hopes and fears about family sessions directly to the therapist (in the presence of the key nurse instead of via the key nurse) and also allowing the therapist to clarify that she has heard Ashleigh's concerns but cannot take the initiative in raising these issues without Ashleigh raising them first, at a time and stage of the family session(s) when she will know it is right for her.

However, in this conversation the therapist makes an opportunity to frame a dilemma that she sees for Ashleigh in having heard her comments about the family sessions, as follows: if

Ashleigh waits long enough for the "right" time, she might feel strong enough (then) to face the consequences of telling her family about her difficulties in relation to them—but if she waits "too long", she continues to sacrifice her "full"/free life while trapped in the "hospital patient/anorexic" role and in family sessions that fall very far short of addressing the important issues for herself and her family to think about and work on.

The family sessions continued, with Ashleigh gradually showing more confidence to speak her mind in family sessions and to use to them to raise potential areas of difference between herself and her family, including differences from her siblings.

The richness of the nurses' and other disciplines' intimate daily knowledge of the children's/young people's lives on the ward creates an entirely different level, compared with outpatient work, of potential "intimacy" within the family therapy. The supervisor and team need to address issues of ethical practice in thinking about the appropriateness of including intimate knowledge about the details of the child's or young person's life in the context of family therapy.

In an outpatient setting, family members have a high degree of control and choice in the level of detailed knowledge of their lives that the therapist will have access to. In the ward situation, the child or young person has far less control and choice and so may be vulnerable to staff's knowledge being shared inappropriately in the team or in the session.

On the other hand, one of the difficulties of working therapeutically with children and young people who are suffering from anorexia is that their condition has a tendency to give rise to behaviours that are "hidden" and experienced as shameful, such as secret vigorous exercising (to "burn off" extra calories) or food-hiding/vomiting after meals, to avoid the feared intake of calories. These behaviours would be seen by staff as relevant material that the child/young person would usefully include in family sessions, whereas the child/young person often prefers to keep such information as a private issue and not to be included in sessions, with counter-therapeutic effects.

The weighing-up of the management of appropriate levels of individual privacy as against the introduction of unhelpful secrecy is a constant ethical-practice issue to which supervisor and team must pay regular attention.

The multidisciplinary team will often be caught up in divisions and dilemmas of whether to privilege the "rights of the child" (i.e. for privacy, autonomy) against the therapeutic aims of the unit (involving bringing in issues of ward-based behaviours, painful family issues that are hard to face, etc.), or vice versa.

Vignette 4

Julia is an 11-year-old girl who has been admitted with low weight and delayed growth. The medical diagnostic label that has been attached to her difficulties is "Food Avoidance Emotional Disorder" (FAED)—a condition thought to affect children where emotionally upsetting experiences are seen to lead to loss of appetite, nausea, and vomiting with concomitant serious weight loss and malnutrition.

Julia is the middle child of three, with an older sister and younger half-brother, all of whom live with both her parents on a deprived west London housing estate. There is a history of Julia having been the object of bullying in school, and her parents have also described their recent traumatic bereavement of their sister/sister-in-law (Julia's maternal aunt) as a trigger factor, in their view, of Julia's eating difficulties.

Julia generally has difficulty speaking in family therapy, is often curled up in a foetal position in sessions, and equally dislikes being the focus of the other family members' conversation in her presence.

The family are due to come for family therapy on a Monday morning, following Julia having had a weekend at home on leave from the ward. (Weekend leave is a routine part of the programme as children begin to recover, with family sessions geared to addressing reintegration and eating-management problems at home, as the child starts to make a graduated return to her or his parents).

One of the nurses from the ward is a member of the family therapy team and has just received "hand-over" information that on, Julia's return to the ward for breakfast, she is upset, unable to eat, and has been saying to her key nurse that the weekend was horrible, that her mother got drunk on Saturday night and then her parents had a row, which ended in physical fighting. She also implies that this regularly happens on Saturday nights.

The supervisee has an established pattern of beginning family sessions by giving the family the opportunity to say how the session should be used and creating their own family therapy "agenda". In the pre-session discussion, the new information that there may be family violence and child-protection issues to be addressed in the family is polarizing team discussion.

Some team members are saying that Julia cannot always be believed—how can we raise it if we don't know it is true? Isn't it for social services to investigate rather than us? Others are saying that we can't move forward with other topics that the family may bring when this key issue is hanging in the air, unspoken about. Others say we should give them the "benefit of the doubt" and let them tell us about it in their own time.

The supervisor is again challenged by a contradiction between "co-constructed" supervisory strategies in which the supervisee's preference for a continuity in her approach to sessions (i.e. giving the family maximum choice for the content of the sessions) is in conflict with the supervisor's belief that child-protection issues cannot be expected to "evolve" in sessions as other family matters might (i.e. that the supervisee will need to find some opportunity to raise this ward-based information with them and also consider whether and how best to contact social services about it).

In addition, the supervisor is wondering whether an unrevealed family-violence pattern may be a significant preserving and maintaining factor in Julia's eating disorder, and whether without addressing these issues we may be in a treatment-without-end that will not be effectively helping the child or her family.

For example, if Julia's parents believe that they should keep their weekend drinking behaviours hidden from the professionals' knowledge, there will be scant possibility of including these issues and how they affect Julia's emotional well-being and eating problems in a discussion with the family about helping Julia move forward, regain weight, and stay well in the future.

The supervisee is also understandably concerned at a potential change in her relationship with the family if she raises unwelcome issues (drinking behaviour and violence) rather than responding to their family preoccupations and supporting them in helping Julia with her eating disorder.

The skills, confidence, and competence to integrate a respectfully challenging approach, maintain a therapeutic alliance, and raise potentially statutory issues (which the family may not know Julia has voiced) are not easily acquired at the early stages of supervised family therapy practice, and yet a "leap" needs to be made.

After extended team discussion, the supervisor and supervisee agreed that the session could begin with the usual "open" framework, including questions about how the weekend had gone, but that at an early stage, if the family did *not* volunteer the information about the story that Julia had articulated to staff on the ward, the supervisee would intervene and raise it as a dilemma—on the one hand, we, as a team, always see it as vital to listen and respond to children's versions of events; on the other, this is new information about a range of difficulties in the family which we haven't heard before and is surprising to us, given our previous knowledge of and relationship with the family (i.e. they had always appeared open with us about what was happening at home). This would be raised in the context of earlier discussions with the family about the "open" team way in which we work—that is, that we include ward-based information in family sessions and also that we can use family meetings as a springboard for raising issues with ward staff, where that is seen by the family as helpful.

It was understood that this kind of conversation between the supervisee and the family may need an extra level of supervisory intervention and support compared with the pattern of supervisory input in previous sessions (i.e. more phone contact, more breaks for the supervisee to come out for discussion, and, if absolutely necessary, the supervisor to join the supervisee in the room).

The intense supervisory process felt thorough and well resolved prior to the appointment time. However, the family (as had often been the case on previous occasions) did not attend and sent no message. The clinical team as a whole decided to invite the parents in for a review of Julia's progress in the light of her distressed state after the weekend, and it was in this context (i.e. parent review meeting rather than family therapy session) that the "professionals' dilemma" issues were able to be put to the parents and explored further.

OVERVIEW

The transposing of collaborative, co-constructed, non-didactic, and conversational approaches to family therapy supervision into the context of inpatient treatment services for child and adolescent eating disorders, where the life-threatening nature of the primary problem cannot be overlooked, poses unique tensions.

The skill of the supervisor in creating a safe-enough environment for the necessary risk-taking of the supervisee in order for her or his practice to develop will be taxed to the limit, alongside pressing claims for "life-saving" interventions into the child and family's life.

The overall context of the team work, and the supervisor's agency-based allegiance to the core task (addressing the eating disorder as a matter of some urgency), may play into the supervisor's natural preference for their own versions of "best practice" in the session(s) and militate against the use of a preferred supervisory style of experimentation, openness to alternatives, and playfulness in the work.

Supportive team relationships and regular consultation to the supervisor are important safeguards against this tendency.

The first clinical vignette (Sarah) illustrates the "pacing" tensions of matching the supervisee's practice developmental choices with the clinical demands of an effective, good-enough family-therapy experience; it also illustrates the supervisor's dilemma in marrying responsible practice with respecting the understandable, possibly unavoidable, supervisee hesitation.

The last clinical vignette (Julia) shows both the specifics of the inpatient setting and its fine-grain knowledge of the child/young person's daily life, as well as highlighting a more common therapy and supervision problem of how to integrate the acknowledgement of child-protection material into therapeutic work, in safe and creative ways.

I would argue, however, that addressing the contradictions inherent in the supervision of this particular highly specialist area of family therapy work helps to shed much light on other, common, issues in both supervision and practice in a postmodern therapy era, where "hard knowledge" is increasingly under scrutiny and open to question.

CHAPTER 8

Working in the grey zone: the challenge for supervision in the area between therapy and social control

Jørn Nielsen

As a supervisor, one encounters many different kinds of therapeutic dilemmas and problems occurring in a plethora of therapeutic contexts, many of which exist within the public-service sector. Most of the cases concern people and families where therapy, in the main, addresses what may be termed communication problems in relationships and aims to provide ways in which clients can move forward with more effective ways of managing their lives. Such cases often do not create great doubt and worries as long as therapy and other kinds of social intervention seem to work to the benefit of the clients and the professional network. Furthermore, cases where, for instance, children are obviously being abused and neglected do not leave much doubt in terms of action required: social control often needs to be taken at times to protect the weak and the vulnerable.

However, other cases are characterized by often highly expressed worries about children and families at risk. Very often the social welfare system and other public agencies are concerned about the child's well-being, parental skills, the quality and stability of daily life, and the interactions between the child, parents, and significant people in the larger context of the child's life. These cases, frequently raise dilemmas of doubt for professionals as to whether therapy and other social interventions can give enough support to aid an improvement in the family situation or whether social control would be a more effective action to take in the interests of the child.

Supervising this type of case puts the supervisor in an important role. The cases are a significant challenge to the supervisor's thinking, skill, and personal style. This chapter addresses systemic ways of analysing and supervising cases in the area between therapy and social control—an area I shall call the grey zone. I would suggest that most literature on supervision does not address this grey zone and thus, in general, does not fully explore supervisor responsibility.

The ideas presented here arise out of my work with

- family centres, to which families are referred by the social services system in order to improve the function of the family, often through attempts to increase parental skills as a means of assuring the professionals of the future safety of the child
- social services agencies, where social workers and case administrators ask for supervision of difficult cases
- psychiatric hospitals and community outpatients psychiatric services
- institutions dealing with the treatment of alcohol and drug abuse
- institutions and professionals dealing with psychological assessments.

Issues for supervisees working in the grey zone

The main issues for supervisees working in the grey zone are outlined below and are also shown diagrammatically in Figure 8.1.

- *Evaluation and examination*—in relation to the family, the therapeutic relationship, and the wider professional network.
- *Therapy and consultation* as ongoing processes and which aim to

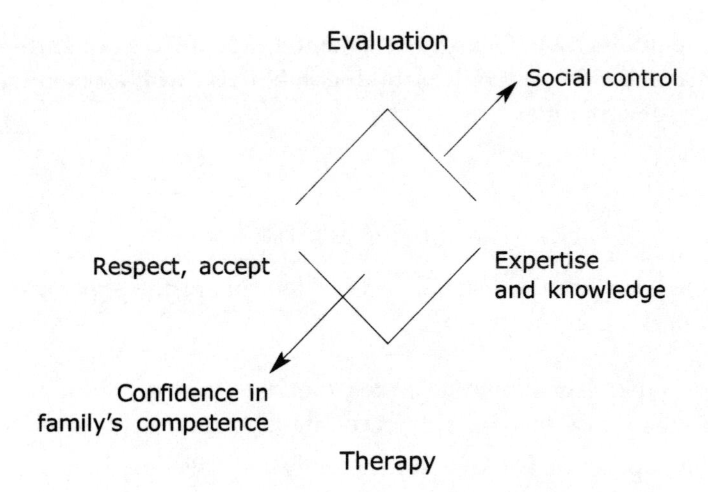

FIGURE 8.1 Issues for supervisees in the grey zone (after Hertz & Nielsen, 1999)

develop the resources of the child, the family, and the larger social context.

- *Social control*—when it should be used, when it should not be used.
- *Trust and belief* in the child's, the family's, and the social system's competence and possibilities as necessary attitudes in order to avoid stigmatizing, to build relationships, and to create possibilities for change and development.
- *Expertise and special knowledge* on child development, risk factors, and methods of intervention.
- *Acknowledgement and respect* for the family's and the social context's way of functioning and organizing together with acceptance of, but not necessarily agreement with, their ideas, knowledge, and belief systems.

While most of these issues are important in any supervisory relationship, they are *all* crucial for supervision in the grey zone. The supervisor needs to recognize these issues and to create a safe and encouraging space, a dialogical arena, where each of the issues in specific cases can be discussed. The supervisor is often working indirectly with large and potentially confusing systems—systems embedded not only with doubt, but also with a potential clashing of certainties.

The supervisor's role

The following are the main aspects of the role of the supervisor when working in the grey zone:

- The supervisor should help the supervisee to always be aware of where case management accountability resides.
- The supervisor has the responsibility to challenge the dominant thinking in relation to both the supervisee and the wider system.
- In such large, complex systems, the supervisor has a responsibility to introduce the voice of others, particularly marginalized voices. Supervising in this way opens up the possibility of bringing in new positions and perspectives, in terms of both clinical work and supervision itself. Other voices could be, for example, the voice of the child, the voice of suppressed hope, the voices of the past, or the voices of successful ideas and proven competencies.
- The supervisor should own his or her expertise and knowledge and introduce these as ideas that may be helpful to the dilemmas that the supervisee brings. These ideas are not a form of absolute proof but ideas for reflection and consideration.

Furthermore, the supervisor can explore with the supervisee the following aspects:

- How the supervisee has dealt with doubt in respect of other complex cases.
- What this has taught the supervisee about his or her own competencies and blind spots.
- The way the supervisee's theoretical orientation might be both helping and constraining the work with the family and the larger system.

- How the supervisor can acknowledge and support the efforts of the supervisee while at the same time being able to constructively challenge him or her.
- Working in the grey zone requires supervisors and clinicians to be able to deal with high levels of tension, both within the therapeutic work and within the professional-network system. It is a central task of the supervisor to help the supervisee explore his or her ability to handle these high levels of tension, and as a contribution to this exploration the supervisor should be clear about his or her own responsibilities and views on working in "the grey zone".

Supervising in the grey zone: examples from practice

Supervising cases in the grey zone requires that they are analysed and understood in the social and cultural contexts within which they exist. These contexts are forever changing, and it is suggested that the supervisor needs to be generally orientated in these contexts and should be able to bring them into the reflecting process of the supervision and as frames for the supervisee's thinking.

Some essential issues are mentioned here and illustrated with examples (see also Nielsen, 1998):

Doubt

In working with psychosocial problems, one will often find a so-called "utopia of wisdom"; this idea is based on the assumption that if one is skilled enough and well-qualified enough to describe, analyse, and evaluate, doubt will disappear. However, in working and supervising in the grey zone, no matter how qualified we become there will always be doubt present as a substantial issue. In supervision, one needs to create a setting and a space for dialogue about the supervisee's doubt and his or her thinking about doubt. Doubt is here seen as the supervisee's state of mind from where reflections and dialogue can rise. When one is being doubtful, it is important to have a contextual frame within which this doubt can be verbalized, examined, and elaborated upon. Supervision is such a context where different premises can be clarified and where marginalized voices can be heard. (See also Börjeson & Håkansson, 1998; Egelund, 1997; Højholt, 1993.)

In technical terms, group supervision seems to be effective through using the techniques of the reflecting team (Andersen, 1994) as a basic model, and from this creative variations can develop:

- Group members can debate questions connected to the doubt.
- Group members can take different positions and speak from their different points of views. This could be by introducing the voice of others as a way of bringing in new positions and perspectives in the supervision—for instance, the voice of the child, the voice of suppressed hopes, the voice of the past, the voice of successful ideas.
- Group members can ask questions or give suggestions.
- Group members can introduce expert views as ideas.
- Group members can introduce different contexts that could clarify and bring meaning to dilemmas.
- Group members can clarify and challenge the supervisees' personal, attitudinal and theoretical preferences as well as institutional values and preferences,

In this way, the reflections of the group members as well of the supervisor introduce a collaborative and co-constructive way for supervisees to develop constructive ways forward in their work.

Example

Susan is a family therapist working with a family where the mother with a 5-year-old daughter is having a severe alcohol problem. It is being reported that the mother is frequently late in picking up her child from the kindergarten, and quite often the child is not fed or properly dressed when she is brought by the mother in the morning. On the other hand, it is seen that the mother also has a caring and warm relationship with her daughter. Susan brings this case and her dilemma to supervision in a group of five therapists and a supervisor.

Susan is quite doubtful as to whether her therapeutic sessions with the mother and child are helpful or not, and she wonders if the therapy is seen as a legitimization of the mother's drinking habits. She is also worried that she will later be blamed for not taking action and expressing her worries to the social services agencies in time, most likely with the consequence of the removal of the daughter from home.

When interviewed about this by the supervisor, Susan explains that the reason she not has reported her worries to the social services agency is that she frequently sees the warm bond between the mother and the child and is still hoping that this bond will continue to improve. Responding to a question from the supervisor, Susan says: "I'm just not sure if the daughter can wait till the mother becomes stable—I mean, a child also needs food, clean clothing, and so on, doesn't it?"

After this, the supervisor clarifies an important dilemma that Susan has recognized: on the one hand, the obvious neglect from the mother; on the other, the hope and wish for the improvement of the mother–child relationship. In other words, the dilemma is between therapeutic work and social control. Susan says spontaneously: "This dilemma is making it very difficult for me—I just don't know which side to choose."

Following this, the supervisor asked each member of the group to ask Susan one question each. Susan was then free to follow the line of any question that she felt would be useful to her. Two questions from the group seemed to be important to her:

- "Do you have to choose between the two sides of the dilemma, or can they co-exist?"
- "Who would you need to contact in order feel more safe about not being blamed later?"

The supervisor interviews Susan about these two questions. In the interview it becomes clear that Susan has the strong belief that she has to choose between continued therapy or social control.

The first question from the group and the following interview by the supervisor challenged the premise that she had to choose between the two sides of the dilemma. It clarified and reframed her thinking that the two sides of the dilemma could coexist and be complementary. A useful dialogue about the two sides would benefit from openness, so Susan decided that she needed to be open about this to the mother as well as to the social services agency. She also felt sure that her relationship to the mother was strong enough to enable her to openly discuss the two sides of the dilemma and Susan's own doubt with her. Susan said: "Discussing this with the mother might even make her trust me more; probably she already knows that I'm doubtful, and being open about it might show me as more trustworthy. I also need to express to her how serious I see the situation as well as how I see her qualities as a mother."

The second question from the group and the following discussion with the supervisor focused on how Susan could feel safer about not being blamed for having withheld worries from the social services agency. In the interview, the supervisor asked about Susan's previous experiences, and it emerged that some years previously she had worked with a similar case. At that time, she was blamed for not having reported child neglect to the social service agencies early enough. It had been a very stressful period to her, and not for any money did she want it repeated. Susan was clearly quite affected when talking about this matter from the past.

The supervisor asked the group members to share their thoughts and experiences with each other about similar cases, and Susan was offered the chance to listen to this for as long as she wanted. The group expressed a recognition and some previous experiences of doubt about when to report worries. One of the members referred to some instances where she frequently met with the social services agency to discuss this doubt openly.

Here Susan broke in and said: "Thank you, this gives me an idea. After talking to the mother, I should meet with her and the social service agency so that my doubt can come out openly. Doing that in time will make it clear to all of us if there is a space for continued therapy, if other support systems are needed, and/or if other interventions should be taken. I think that the mother as well as others has a right to express their thinking and to get information about the state of the process. Hopefully this can lead to a common plan where we're working together and not seeing each other as opponents."

Susan then developed the idea of inviting the mother, the daughter, the social worker, and the staff to a consultation where the situation and the doubt could be discussed.

Marginalizing of groups at risk

In Denmark, as well as in other Western countries, many people are able to develop and live to the fullest of their potential, but a certain percentage of the population experiences severe difficulties, feels excluded, and could be said to be in a situation characterized by a risk of further marginalization (Jørgensen et al., 1993). For example, children with difficulties may be placed in special educational settings, excluded from public-school settings, removed from home, and deprived of the possibility of interaction with their ordinary peers. The problems these children exhibit become visible usually in their early years and then continue to be problematic. Quite often such children show severe behavioural problems, criminality, and, later, drug abuse. Obviously, these children and young people are in a context where social control and extensive arrangements for the child are often considered.

Most professionals involved in work with children claim that they work to ensure the welfare of the children—yet it is known that children's voices and wishes are often not heard (Egelund, 1997). The same can be said of the families of such children, and research shows that many families dependent on the social welfare system are in a situation where they are being overruled, disengaged from their own resources, and perceived as lacking resources (Uggerhøj, 1995).

These children and their families are often characterized by the paradox that very often they are not welcome in "ordinary" settings, and yet at the same time they need a close involvement with significant adults and "ordinary" settings. These marginalized groups are frequently the subject of intense political discussion: how do we treat these groups, how does society protect itself from the assaults from these young citizens, where do we place them? In other words, these groups become victims of the process of "othering": "What do *we* do with *them?*"

Supervisees working in the grey zone find themselves in this field, where marginalization is a strong subject. In supervision, marginalization and the possibilities of integration and creating a developmental environment for the child have to be addressed. The political aspects and the current trends in the social welfare system should be addressed and challenged in order to clarify the situation and the possibilities. Also, the understanding of marginalizing forces and of marginalized voices—for example, the child's—need to be addressed in order to develop new understandings and premises.

Example

Claus is a social worker working with the Jensen family. The two sons aged 12 and 16 years are showing severe behavioural problems including theft and violence. The sons have a long history of placements in different schools, and previously they have been placed in two different foster families. The children are again living with their parents, but the teachers at school are again strongly suggesting that the boys be removed from home and school. The school has written to the parents as well as to the social services agency and said that it is "the last chance" for the two young boys. Claus's thinking is—and the father has the same view—that if the two sons are removed again, the situation will only become worse.

During the initial discussion in the group supervision, the supervisor asks the crucial question: who has the problem? The discussion clarifies for Claus that recognition and understanding of the school's and the teachers' positions are important. The supervisor develops a line of questioning that addresses the kind of help and information that the school has received so far, and it becomes clear to Claus that the school has not been informed and supported sufficiently in the past and that the contact between the parents, the boys, and the teachers is weak and unstable. Claus adds that he himself has disagreed so strongly with the school's attitudes that he has neglected their position and concerns.

The group is then asked to reflect on what they have heard. In this reflection, three themes come up:

- The relationship between Claus and the school system is important, but in fact it is weak and unstable.
- The boys' wishes seem to have been overlooked.
- The relationships between the parents and the school system is, for the moment, based on suspicion and hostility.

The supervisor asks Claus to rank the importance of these themes, and to Claus it becomes apparent that both the teachers, the sons, and the parents are—from different perspectives— at risk of being marginalized and overlooked.

Claus also becomes aware that he himself has contributed to this by not having paid attention to the school system and also by not having created space in which the sons' voices could be heard. He ranks in matter of importance that he should first work on establishing a space where the idea of supporting the school system can be developed. If the school system is not supported and recognized, the attitudes of the teachers towards the boys will only become more unfriendly—the opposite of what is needed. Second, he needs to work on establishing a dialogue between the sons and the teachers trying to build up a mutual project of responsibility for the situation at school. Third, he would like all parties—the sons, the parents, and the teachers—to get together to find a common understanding of the whole situation.

This leads—after a reflection from the group—to the idea that Claus's goal should be to establish a consultation with the family and school systems which would explore, in particular, what the school needs from the parents, from the children, and from others in order to continue working with the boys.

The supervisor asks: "What would be best for you: to meet with the different subsystems first or to have this consultation with all the parties at once?" After a while, Claus says: "Well, I have a tendency to meet with subsystems before having a consultation with everyone involved. But thinking it over, I think that in this case there are so many different viewpoints that I'd prefer to see them all at once. Maybe that's also what the boys are trying to tell me with their behaviour. At least I'm pretty sure that everybody will show up if I invite them. Then all different questions and perspectives can be clarified."

Politicization of the clinical and social field

In an increasing way, the social and clinical field is becoming a subject for political debate. This debate influences the law, the interpretation of the law, and the specific way of working in public agencies. The supervisor needs to be aware of this and to include and discuss the supervisee's ethical, moral, and political thinking as part of the supervision process (Hertz & Nielsen, 1999; Münster & Schmidt, 1997).

Psychosocial problems exists in a complex context. The different participants often have different viewpoints. This brings a situation where conflicts and different values, evaluations, and clinical attitudes are what the supervisee meets and brings to the supervision.

In supervision, the influence of current political debate should be addressed and discussed openly. Becoming aware of the impact of this larger political context enables the supervisee to integrate this in a balanced and reflected way.

Example

John is a psychologist working with so-called multi-problems families. He is in contact with a number of cases of children who are in very under-stimulating environments, and he often has real doubts as to whether he should suggest that a child should be removed from home or if he should continue to contribute to the establishment of a nurturing environment for the child at home.

In an individual supervision, he brings up that lately he has noticed an increasing tendency in his work to recommend removal of number of children at risk—which, he says, he wouldn't have done half a year ago. He wonders why. So what he brings to supervision is not related to a specific case but is more related to a theme: why has he, in half a year, developed an increased tendency to report and suggest to social services agencies that children should be removed and social control be considered?

John is quite experienced in working with this type of case, and he is very much aware that in his position he is dealing with issues of doubt, professional and personal judgement, and power. Still, he wonders why there has been an increase in his own tendency to suggest removal of children from home instead of trying to work with empowerment and building on the families resources.

The supervisor asks John why he has become aware of this tendency now. John immediately responds that he has been thinking about this since it became clear to his mind that currently the newspapers are filled with examples and cases of children exposed to child abuse and neglect. Following these examples in the media, many politicians and experts on child care and protection are claiming that the public-welfare systems are taking the wishes of the parents too much into consideration compared to the consideration of the child's welfare.

The supervisor asks John how he feels about this debate in the media, and he responds that he is very ambivalent but that in the main he thinks that these case are so complex that it is difficult to generalize about them as many politicians and experts tend to do. John is also convinced that when people recommend to the social services systems more and earlier removals of children, they are frequently doing so in order to assure themselves and others that they are responsible and working for the benefit of the children. He feels that there is a lack of focus on cases where parents have managed to develop parental skills through therapy and social support.

The supervisor expresses the idea that John is being affected by this debate to a wider extent than he was actually aware of, and that to some extent he is afraid of being isolated because of his viewpoints.

This idea makes a lot of sense to John. He explains that previously he frequently discussed political and social issues with his colleagues and with the managers in his department. Recently he has become very quiet and low profiled in these matters, and now he is sure that this has to with a fear of being isolated because of his non-mainstream ideas. He also recalls that previously he had been quite isolated in his department as a result of some of his ideas on how to do therapy with families, and this history of professional isolation was quite uncomfortable to him. Prompted by the supervisor, he remembers further that he has also gained quite a bit of recognition in raising professional and political questions.

During the session it becomes clear that he needs to negotiate this theme with his manager and his colleagues. He creates the idea that he will invite them to an open debate where he will tell them about what he has noticed about his own tendencies and reactions and will invite his colleagues to reflect on this and to share their own experiences. As he says: "When I'm influenced by the current debate, why wouldn't the rest of my colleagues be?"

The supervisor asks John what he expects from this debate. John says that he has no specific goal other than creating a space where these political and mainstream ideas and their impact on the professional work can be discussed. The objective of this is to break his own isolation because of his viewpoints and to clarify to the whole staff that political tendencies have an impact on professional work—not least in cases embedded with doubt and low predictability.

The supervisor supports John's idea and adds a suggestion that John and his colleagues could also discuss and share their ideas about how they see their own positions as professionals in the area between therapy and social control and how they deal with the expectations and power connected to these position. He suggests that these professional narratives about administration of power will bring new perspectives and professional understandings into the group. John nods his head in agreement with this suggestion.

System-knowledge and system-orientation as a necessity

In the most difficult cases, many professionals and professional disciplines are involved—teachers, nurses, social workers, psychologists, doctors, and so on. They create, together with the family, the most important context for understanding the problems and for the development of constructive interventions. The number of people involved can be quite high, and the task of coordination, coexistence, and co-creation of the efforts is a challenge in itself.

The cooperation and the relationships between the participating public agencies are often characterized by a lack of knowledge of each other's areas of competence, traditions, and ways of understanding. This can be a source for mistrust, prejudice, and scepticism in the public network (Højholt, 1993; Imber-Black, 1988; Mielcke, 1998). Many social interventions are carried out on a basis of traditions and assumptions. The underlying thinking and the theoretical and empirical validation of this can be challenged and reformulated (Börjeson & Håkansson, 1998).

Supervisees often find themselves in this arena of multiple professionals and multiple agencies.

The supervisor in the grey zone therefore needs to have an overview of the wider professional-network system, its way of functioning and organizing, legal background, area of competence, traditions, methods, values, and code of ethics. The supervisor must ensure that the supervisee is given the opportunity to think about this wider context and thus develop a greater range of possible interventions. Mapping techniques and genograms are frequently useful in helping the supervisee get an overview of the larger system.

CONCLUSION

At a time when, throughout Europe, there is an increasing emphasis in therapeutic work on accountability and the monitoring of good practice, it is clear that supervision is becoming more and more a substantial tool for attempting to guarantee the quality of work offered by therapists and others in the helping profession. Quality supervision is even more crucial in the grey-zone area between therapy and social control. A central issue, therefore, has to be a clarity around the mandate for supervision, for a lack of clarity about these matters will inevitably lead to a lack of good practice and ultimately contribute to those who already have marginalized voices finding themselves less and less heard.

CHAPTER 9

"But how can I help if I don't know?" Supervising work with refugee families

Renos K. Papadopoulos

In supervising work with refugees, I am frequently asked by therapists and other workers how they can be helpful if they do not "know" much about their refugee clients. This, of course, is a legitimate concern. Therapists should always know enough about the people they work with. However, it seems to me that this question, in this particular context, has wider ramifications: it raises a host of issues connected with the *type* and *amount* of "knowledge" that therapists and, in general, refugee workers think they must have in order to feel confident in working with their refugee clients. Moreover, it is also important to ponder on how the choice of the *type* and *amount* of this "knowledge" is made.

Refugees and systems

People have always moved from one territory to another when they felt threatened, but the phenomenon of refugeedom is a relatively recent one, arising from when ethnic groups, nations, and states developed their own discrete boundaries (Black &

Koser, 1999; Carlier & Vanheule, 1997; Hampton, 1998; Joly, 1996; Kushner & Knox, 1999; Loescher, 1993). Refugees tend to evoke strong reactions, both positive and negative. People in the receiving country sway between two opposite sets of feelings towards them: compassion for having lost their homes, and fear that the refugees' presence may adversely affect their own lives. For example, when Bosnian refugees came to the U.K. in the early to mid-1990s, they were welcomed most warmly but also, in some places, met with hostility because they were seen as being given priority over the local population in terms of resources such as health and housing. Thus, allowing refugees to enter a country does not only represent a humanitarian act but also involves a great many other considerations.

The phenomenon of refugeedom intersects a wide variety of dimensions, and by no means is it exclusively of a psychological nature; it involves issues of a political (internal party politics as well as foreign policy), ethical, ethnic, religious, financial, sociological, or ecological nature, to name but a few. Consequently, a single approach to refugees cannot possibly be sufficient to address its multifaceted complexity. Therefore, any psychological-therapeutic approach to refugees should include a means of taking into consideration the other interrelated dimensions, and it is for this reason that a systemic perspective can be particularly apt for this kind of work. More specifically, some of the advantages of a systemic approach in working with refugees include the ability to address several interrelated systems as well as to avoid the pathologizing of refugee suffering or the psychologizing of evil actions as in political decisions and actual atrocities (Papadopoulos & Hildebrand, 1997). The interrelated systems in this work include the systems where the clients belong—that is, the nuclear and extended family, the school, the community, the ethnic, cultural, and linguistic group, and the state—and the systems that form the relevant context—that is, sociopolitical, ideological, ethical, and religious systems, as well as the media, "public opinion", and so on. Moreover, the systemic approach can be particularly useful in enabling therapists to locate themselves in the context of the service systems where they belong and as they interact with the other two groups of systems. The therapists' systems include the actual services and institutions where they are employed, along with their policies and practices, the ideologies of the aid industry, professional affiliations, therapeutic orientation, as well as their own personal background and history. Finally, systemic approaches are useful in working with refugees because they can sharpen the professionals' epistemological sensitivity and inform them about the interaction of the various narratives that each one of these systems uses to express itself (Papadopoulos, 1999a).

The noise that makes a difference

One of the main principles of systemic thinking, as applied to psychotherapeutic work, has been the distinction between information and data. According to Bateson's famous dictum, "information is definable as a difference which makes a difference" (1971, p. 315). This means that not everything that a therapist hears in a session or learns from the referring network matters or is helpful to the therapeutic process; thus, therapists attempt to discern the relevant information from the background noise, from all the data that tend to overload them without offering clarity that would be useful to the therapeutic work. The key to this discrimination is based on the feedback process: therapists endeavour to watch out for evidence of a difference in the way they understand the family system—and in the way they interact with the family—after they become aware of a certain piece of information. For example, after hearing about the fact that a member of a refugee family was tortured, the therapist may actively seek to understand the way that he or she now perceives the family differently and the ways that their interaction has been affected as a result of this new information. Needless to say, this awareness develops not only when therapists hear passively or observe something that comes from the family accidentally, but also when they themselves actively seek it out—their questions, interventions, and overall position contribute to the elicitation of relevant information and a decrease of the noise produced by background data. In this way, one of the main functions of supervision is precisely to develop the therapists' skills to discriminate between information and data and to increase their effectiveness in eliciting appropriate information.

Although the Batesonian terminology about difference, information, and background noise is not used widely in current systemic thinking and practice, nevertheless the ideas that it conveys are valid and seem to remain, by and large, widely accepted. Every therapeutic approach and technique aims to maximize whatever it considers relevant information and to minimize the interference from background noise. However, what is perhaps more important about the distinction between information and data is what Bateson said about the noise itself. After clarifying that "All that is not information . . . is noise", he characterized the noise as "the only possible source of *new* patterns" (1967, p. 410). This is a rather astonishing comment about the noise and its potential value. What this means is that by pursuing what we perceive as relevant information, we tend to ignore other possible avenues that could reveal new patterns that could lead to creative ways of appreciating the situation. Understandably, the emphasis on the positive use of information has tended to downgrade the value of the background noise, and it is astounding to read that Bateson appreciated it as the "possible source of *new* patterns". Although it may be relatively easy to accept the value of this kind of noise on the theoretical level, it may be less obvious how this can be translated in the actual therapeutic work. Moreover, what could this potentially creative noise that makes a difference be in the context of working with refugees, and how can we access it?

To begin with, it may be useful to differentiate between at least two types of background noise: one that emerges within the session, and another that is part of the wider contexts within which the therapeutic work takes place. The two, of course, are interconnected. The first one refers to a micro-level, and it consists of all the specific background data about the clients and therapists that may not be considered of relevance in comparison to the focused information that is pursued; for example, the fact that a refugee family had two dogs and a cat back at home may not be perceived relevant by the therapist who is focusing, at the time, on the father's difficulties in adjusting to the family's new life in the U.K. The second type of background noise refers to a macro-level and it consists of the wider narratives in the sociopolitical contexts; for example, the fact that the Indian authorities use the term "militancy" rather than "terrorism" to refer to the actions of secessionist groups in their subcontinent. This fact may not be of relevance to the therapeutic work with the refugee family from that region unless it is specifically focused upon.

Therapists and refugee workers, like all other citizens, are exposed to the wider societal narratives about refugees that address not only the psychological plight of the fleeing people but also a host of other aspects of the whole mosaic that contains the refugee condition. Among the many narratives of this kind, perhaps the most relevant ones are the versions of the dominant stories about the political and military conflict that forced these people to become refugees, and the versions of the receiving country's attitude towards that particular group of asylum seekers.

Within the last decade, our world has been overwhelmed by images of destruction in several parts of the world: Azerbaijan, Georgia, Armenia, Croatia, Bosnia, Rwanda, Chechnya, Kosovo, Timor, to name the main ones. Inevitably, the specific range of positions (political, strategic, moral, financial, etc.) that each country adopts in relation to each one of these conflicts affects the framework within which therapists formulate their own work with refugees from that conflict zone. Although health-care workers respond professionally to their clients, inevitably the wider societal narratives impact on the specific ways that their response is formulated. Ultimately, it is unavoidable that the overall political climate affects the ways that professionals perceive and carry out their roles in relation to refugee care (cf. Papadopoulos, 1997, 1998, 2000a, 2000b; Papadopoulos & Hildebrand, 1997; Preston, 1999; Vernez, 1991).

Thus, Bateson's claim that the noise (in addition to the expected benefits of the focused information) is capable of creating new patterns can be of great value to the practical context of refugee work. This means that not only the focused information that is addressed intentionally in therapy but also the wider perspectives within which the therapeutic work is located influence what occurs in therapy and how workers and refugees relate to each other. For example, in recent years, Serbian refugees in the U.K. have been living under the cloud of the predominant hostile attitude towards Serbia, and this must have affected their work with therapists. According to this example, although the background noise of the anti-Serbian political climate may not always have been in the forefront of the therapists' and Serbian refugees' consciousness, if focused upon it could have provided new and useful information for the therapeutic encounter.

Moreover, in addition to the various shades of political issues, there is another important domain that seems to determine a therapist's perception as to what is relevant information in working with refugees. This is less tangible but equally, if not more, significant: this is about the wider societal discourse on what could be called "refugee trauma". Much has been written about the controversy about trauma and specifically "refugee trauma" (Arroyo & Eth, 1996; Bentovim, 1992; Caruth, 1996; Eisenbruch, 1991; Friedman & Jaranson, 1992; Gorman, 2000; Herman, 1992; Joseph & Yule, 1997; LaCapra, 2000; Lebowitz & Newman, 1996; Marsella, 1992; Marsella et al., 1996; O'Brien, 1998; Papadopoulos, 1998, 1999b, 2000a, 2000b, in press; Shephard, 2000; Tedeschi & Calhoun, 1995; Yehuda & McFarlane, 1995; Young, 1997; Yule, 1999; Zur, 1996). Papadopoulos and Hildebrand argued that the usual way professionals tend to conceptualize refugees was within a "pathology or deficit model" (1997, p. 209). This echoes similar perspectives developed by other authors (e.g. Bracken & Petty, 1998; Muecke, 1992; Summerfield, 1999, 2001). The trauma discourse in refugees is so widespread that it pervades our whole social fabric. The media, politicians, and the general public have been saturated by the trauma discourse to the extent that all assume that more or less all refugees are "traumatized". The word "trauma" has acquired an almost magic quality because it has an enormous impact on all of us. It tends to mobilize people into action—the public gives money generously to all people who have been "traumatized", politicians take various forms of action (from offering aid to ordering military action) when faced with the movement of massive proportions of "traumatized" population, professionals and services tend to accede to the requests made by or on behalf of "traumatized" persons, and so forth. Inevitably, the pervasive "trauma" discourse forms an unavoidable background noise in every therapeutic endeavour with refugees. In this sense, it could be argued that this particular type of noise would certainly make a difference to the way we work and supervise work with refugees.

The case of Zahra

To illustrate some of these issues, I reproduce below the account of an educational psychologist who asked me to supervise her in connection with a difficult case of a refugee girl she was working with. This is what the psychologist wrote:

> *Background to supervision*
>
> "I decided to contact Professor Papadopoulos because of my concerns about a pupil with whom I was working (whom I will call Zahra), who was not making progress and with whom I felt impotent in my attempts to help. The pupil concerned came to this country as a refugee under traumatic circumstances. As the educational psychologist attached to Zahra's school, I am able to visit the school three times a term. I was asked by her school to assess the impact her previous experiences were having on her life and educational development. Since I felt that my knowledge and experience of working with refugees was limited, and I was interested in finding out more about this area, I approached Professor Papadopoulos in the hope that such supervision might facilitate and enable my work."
>
> *Referral*
>
> "Zahra is a 10-year-old girl who came to this country as a refugee from East Africa when she was 4 years of age. Her first language is not English but a local dialect which she still speaks at home. Zahra came to England in 1995 with her father and sister in order to escape the violence in her country. The tribe to which her family belonged were apparently being very badly treated, and it is thought that Zahra would have been exposed to a high level of trauma and violence there. Her mother was ill at the time of Zahra's departure and was planning to join the rest of the family; however, she died in the refugee camp before she could make the journey to England.
>
> "Zahra now lives with her paternal uncle, his wife, and their own children. Zahra's father still lives in London but looks after her sister who is handicapped. It is unclear why Zahra

does not live with them, but it was suggested that her father could not manage both children himself and therefore asked his brother to care for Zahra. Her father maintains regular contact with Zahra. Zahra's family feel she could not make sense of her mother's death (she was about 4 years old at the time) and say that they have never discussed this with her.

"In school, Zahra's teachers were concerned that, having been in the country for over four years, Zahra was still not speaking at all (at school), nor did she seem able to understand much of what was happening in the classroom. As a consequence, her academic progress was being severely hindered. In referring Zahra to an educational psychologist, the school were particularly concerned that I should address the way in which her traumatic experiences in her country were impacting on her current mental and emotional state, as well as her learning.

"In my initial meeting with Zahra, she presented as being very shy and withdrawn. Despite doing my best to put her at ease, she did not say a word nor did she respond to any of my attempts to make conversation or find out a little bit about her. She smiled and behaved in a cooperative way that left me uncertain about how much she was even able to understand. As I was not able to get a translator who spoke her language, I had to try to communicate with Zahra through the use of gesture and other non-verbal tasks. I knew that most of the assessment materials would be culturally inappropriate, but above all I was struggling to find a way to connect with Zahra as she seemed so distant from everything and everyone around her."

Outcome of supervision

"In my supervision with Professor Papadopoulos, I found myself focusing on how Zahra's experiences as a refugee might be affecting her—thinking about the trauma she must have experienced and how it must be impacting on her life and development. I expressed my sense of being at a loss in terms of how to approach the task of helping her and of trying to assess her skills and functioning in order to engage better with her—academically and emotionally. During the supervision, however, Professor Papadopoulos encouraged me to look beyond the focus on her trauma and think about her as I would any other pupil. He asked me, for instance, how I might work with any other pupil. Thinking about this made me realize that my own preoccupation with her trauma and the impact on her of being a refugee was preventing me from thinking about her in a more holistic way.

"We then considered the range of possible factors that might be affecting her. These included: the cultural differences and deprivation she may be feeling; the loss of both her parents (through death or separation) and her sense of family; possible learning difficulties as well as her exposure to the traumas of war and violence. I realized how easy it had become to focus on one aspect of her history and the supervision was helpful in drawing my attention to the variety of other factors and possible influences contributing to her presentation and difficulties.

"As a result of the supervision and of having had the opportunity to think about my own experience of working with Zahra, I was also enabled to think differently about how Zahra might have been feeling. I wondered for example, whether my sense of isolation in this work, coupled with the extreme difficulties I faced in trying to understand Zahra, might in some way have also reflected Zahra's own sense of loneliness and confusion in trying to make sense of what had happened in her life.

"I am continuing to work with Zahra, her school, and, as far as possible, her family."

Refugee trauma as noise and information

Although, of course, each case has its unique features, Zahra's predicament is fairly typical of the type that I am often called upon to supervise. Whenever persons have a refugee background, however remote, there is a tendency to connect their present difficulties with the fact that originally they came to this country as refugees. Nobody would argue that these two variables may not be connected, but what is important to appreciate is how quickly this connection is made without investigating the specific features and circumstances of each case.

According to Zahra's referral, the school was understandably concerned that her "academic progress was severely hindered". The reason we are given is that she did not speak "at all [at school], nor did she seem able to understand much of what was happening in the classroom". One tangible cause the school saw was that she was a refugee, and "it is thought that Zahra would have been exposed to a high level of trauma and violence there"—that is, in her country of origin—because "the tribe to which her family belonged were apparently being very badly treated". It is interesting to observe that all these connections were formulated in a hypothetical way, and yet they led to a concrete action—a referral to a psychologist to investigate "the way in which her traumatic experiences in her country were impacting on her current mental and emotional state, as well as her learning". What should be of further interest is how the other pieces of information about her life were not taken into consideration at all. I am referring to the fact that this girl of 10 had lost her mother at the age of 4, does not live with her own father but with her paternal uncle and his family, has a "handicapped" sister who is cared for by her father, and seems to be surrounded by adults who do not address these enormous losses in her life. What is also important is that she has been in this country for six years and, despite all her obvious tragic current circumstances, the main attention is turned to the trauma that hypothetically she may have suffered during possible armed conflict in her country of origin.

To date, it has not been established whether Zahra was indeed exposed or not to atrocities in her country. However, what is of note is how easily we tend to use the refugee-trauma hypothesis as the main possible cause and how we tend to discard and assign a background-noise status to other considerations, regardless of their apparent relevance. Trauma seems to offer tangible and clear "evidence", which is most welcome in situations of unclarity, unbearable suffering, and messy feelings and situations.

It is evident that in the case of Zahra, too, refugee trauma was the main focus of investigation on behalf of the school and initially by the educational psychologist. Under closer scrutiny, we may discern a very curious phenomenon. The refugee trauma was the information that the therapeutic work sought to elicit, and yet at the same time it is evident that refugee trauma was the background noise that gave rise to the choice of this focus in the first place. In other words, the macro-level background noise slipped into becoming the main theme of the therapeutic focus. By doing this, it bypassed all other possible and even more obvious foci (e.g. that Zahra lived with another family and not her own and that this fact was not accounted for by anyone). This puzzle is of paramount importance in supervision. By focusing on this very puzzle, the supervisor, in effect, encourages and indeed joins the supervisee in tracing back this process and thus initiates the exploration of the wider narratives within which therapy had been located. More specifically, it is most instructive to observe, in action, how the refugee-trauma narrative shapes the referring network, the therapist, and the supervisor.

In the case of this supervision, although the psychologist/supervisee was expecting a long process of learning about refugees, she was able, after only one session, to realize that her own existing expertise was sufficient to work fruitfully with Zahra. It is as if the background ideology of refugee trauma (as one could call it) had a paralysing effect on her, and, once this was lifted, her own creativity and resourcefulness were unlocked.

What makes refugee trauma have such a powerful effect on therapists? Why and how does refugee trauma acquire such a privileged position, on the one hand, and yet, on the other, operates in an almost imperceptible manner? Before discussing further this case, it would be useful to examine the concept and phenomenon of trauma in general and of refugee trauma in particular.

Trauma—a brief sketch

It is instructive to be reminded that the idea of trauma as a psychological concept was first introduced in the context of insurance claims made by survivors of railway accidents shortly after the first passenger railway line opened (between Liverpool and Manchester) back in 1830. "Trauma" and "traumatic neuroses" emerged as useful psychological categories to account for the somatic symptoms without evident organic origin in accident survivors. With the increase of accidents due to industrialization, "from 1880 onwards, various European countries enacted legislation to provide compensation for traumatically injured workers" (Healy, 1993, p. 90). About the same time, the French psychiatrists Charcot, Bernheim, and Janet investigated the dynamics of traumatic neurosis and traumatic hysteria using hypnosis and suggestion. Both Freud and Jung studied (at different times) these methods in France well before Breuer and Freud introduced trauma as one of the central ideas in the emerging field of psychoanalysis. In their classic text *Studies on Hysteria* (Freud, 1895d), Breuer and Freud elaborated on the proposition that memories of highly emotionally charged experiences were not forgotten but repressed. This gave rise to the psychoanalytic investigations into the dynamics of these psychological mechanisms. The two pioneers of psychoanalysis argued that the repressed material was responsible for the development of later pathological symptoms. The treatment was therefore based on the causal-reductive technique of abreaction, through which one could reconnect with the repressed original emotional response. However, even Breuer and Freud at that time warned against simplistic explanations: "We must not expect to meet with a *single* traumatic memory and a *single* pathogenic idea as its nucleus; we must be prepared for *successions* of *partial* traumas and *concatenations* of pathogenic trains of thought" (Freud, 1895d, pp. 287–288). Yet the refugee-trauma ideology proposes a fairly simplistic connection between the traumatic event and the subsequent psychological consequences, as the case of Zahra exemplified.

Although the traumatic causation of neurosis was one of the first psychoanalytic explanations, it should be remembered that psychoanalysis was able to advance once it abandoned the trauma theory and moved into more sophisticated forms of psychological formation of symptoms; these were based on various interactional models between fantasy and reality, internal drives and societal prescriptions, early relationships with parental figures and later relationships with significant others, defence mechanisms and external reality, and so on. Summing up the course of trauma theory, Anna Freud put it very succinctly:

> A "trauma" or "traumatic happening" meant originally an (external or internal) event of a magnitude with which the

> individual's ego is unable to deal, i.e. a sudden influx of excitation, massive enough to break through the ego's normal stimulus barrier. To this purely quantitative meaning of the term were added in time all sorts of qualifications (such as cumulative, retrospective, silent, beneficial), until the concept ended up as more or less synonymous with the notion of a pathogenic event in general. [quoted in Nagera, 1970, p. 10]

Anna Freud was right when she concluded that trauma no longer had any specific meaning except that of a general reference to a "pathogenic event". I would argue that since the time that she wrote this passage, trauma has become even more vague, and it now refers to anything connected with a strong emotional response. So, what happened to revive this term, which was on its way to extinction? Although this is not the place to develop systematically the historical parameters of this revival, it could be argued that possibly two groups of reasons may be responsible for this: the aftermath of the Vietnam War (and subsequent abhorrence of other military conflicts), and the emerging awareness of child sexual abuse and the concurrent attack on Freud's abandonment of the seduction theory.

The return home of Vietnam veterans not as heroes but as confused victims of the much-criticized U.S. foreign policy forced U.S. professionals to account for the veterans' psychological condition. In other words, if the veterans' war experiences and post-war reactions were to be accounted for within the context of a heroic story, it is less likely that mental health professionals would have been called upon to assist them. Heroes are admired and adored; they are not treated psychologically. Every experience requires a framework within which to be located and assigned meaning, and the wider narratives in the socio-ecology provide such frameworks. In that particular instance, the medicalization and even pathologization of the suffering of the Vietnam veterans enabled the public to assign a specific cluster of meanings to that phenomenon in a most fitting way. More specifically, the trauma narrative was able to encapsulate at least three attitudes—opposition to the Vietnam War, empathy with the suffering soldiers as long as they are defined as patients, and distance from their predicament which others preferred to view as extraordinary and exotic. The trauma narrative and, more specifically, the post-traumatic stress disorder explanation seem to have fitted perfectly with that set of circumstances. Remarkably similar processes were repeated recently, especially with reference to the wars in the territories of the former Yugoslavia, when the public opinion in the West wanted both to condemn the wars and also empathize with the plight of refugees while keeping them at some distance.

The widespread awareness of child sexual abuse in most countries also contributed to the revival of the term "trauma". It was shocking to realize that so many children were abused, and that awareness itself seems to have had a "traumatic" effect on the public. Inevitably, attention turned to Freud who had abandoned his original seduction theory, according to which an actual seduction in childhood was the cause of neurosis in later life. Masson's controversial book, *The Assault on Truth: Freud's Suppression of the Seduction Theory* (1984), attacked Freud for downplaying the theory of the actual traumatic nature of the abuse (by seduction) and, in a sense, argued for the reinstatement of the trauma theory.

Not only within psychoanalysis but also in the systemic field reservations were expressed about the usefulness of trauma theory. As early as 1957, Don Jackson, in his seminal paper "A Note on the Importance of Trauma in the Genesis of Schizophrenia", questioned the validity of identifiable and specific trauma as causal of severe emotional illness. Instead, he proposed that active family interactions, in their complexity and intensity as a continuing condition operating in the person's environment, can offer better explanations for a person's psychological difficulties.

Regardless of the precise nature of the reasons, the trauma theory has recently returned with a vengeance, and it now occupies a central position in the public's way of perceiving various misfortunes. In particular, the refugee-trauma story has acquired undeniable dominance over other possible narratives. At the same time, the critics of its usefulness and application to the refugee situation have continued to be vocal (Bracken & Petty, 1998; Summerfield, 1999, 2001). One of the main difficulties with the idea of "trauma" is that its insistence on referring to a monocausal set of specific historical events downplays the constructivist side of it. In other words, although trauma is essentially a socially constructed concept through various societal narratives and ideologies, its connection to factual events creates a deceptive feeling of factuality about it. Moreover, there is another telling confusion about trauma: trauma as a noun and trauma as an adjective. Logically, trauma refers to the way a person comprehends and accounts for certain experiences, and therefore one would say that certain experiences were traumatic or that certain events were experienced as traumatic. However, in recent years "trauma" has been widely used in an absolute and categorical way to refer to "traumatic events". This means that it is taken for granted that because certain events are painful or reprehensible or violent or unusual, they must have a traumatic impact on those who witness them. This is a very grave epistemological error. It is logically and psychologically erroneous to assume that adverse circumstances always traumatize the persons involved. Such formulation does not allow for variations in human experience, and it pathologizes events without any reference to the ways that individuals and groups process them.

Trauma—etymology and meanings

Before venturing further into the implication of refugee trauma, it would be useful to ponder over its original meaning. Trauma is a Greek word that means a "wound", a "lesion", or an "injury", and it comes from the verb "to pierce" or "to penetrate". However, there is a very important etymological root that has been overlooked by the vast literature on the subject (Papadopoulos, 2000b, in press). This root is the verb *teiro*, which means "to rub", and it is the source of the verb *titrosko*, which means "to pierce". *Teiro* has two different meanings in ancient Greek which could be best rendered in English as "to rub in" and "to rub away" or "to rub off". This means that if something was rubbed onto somebody's skin, it could either pierce it and create a wound (it would have been "rubbed in") or it could erase whatever else was on the skin before (like a rubber erases pencil writing on paper). Thus, according to the original Greek meaning of the word, "trauma is simply the mark left by either a wound (the result of an experience being '*rubbed in*') or a process of cleansing (the result of an experience having '*rubbed* [something] *off*' or '*rubbed* [it] *away*'). Trauma can be the result of an injury or the result of a cleansing" (Papadopoulos,

2000b, p. 93). What is evident from the etymological meanings is that trauma is not necessarily a mark of pathology; it is a neutral word that suggests that a strong emotional experience has taken place and has left some mark—either a mark of injury or of cleansing and renewal. Trauma is the mark, the emblem of that experience regardless of its nature or value, of its positive or negative connotation. Powerful experiences may indeed injure or rejuvenate a person. However, according to our common use of the term today, only the negative connotation has survived, and although it makes perfect sense that a positive outcome may also be the case, it has become impossible for us nowadays to consider anything constructive and affirmative when we think of refugee trauma.

The phases of refugee trauma

As we saw in the case of Zahra, the implicit hypothesis that organized the school's and educational psychologist's thinking and actions was not about her painful experiences of not living with her father and sister, or of losing her mother at an early age, but about the possibility of her witnessing war atrocities. To return to the question asked at the beginning of this chapter—that is, about "the *type* and *amount* of 'knowledge' that therapists . . . think they must have in order to feel confident in working with their refugee clients", it now becomes clearer that therapists, under the background influence of the trauma narrative, seem to be under pressure to tease out the details of the trauma that is assumed to have been caused by the refugees' exposure to war atrocities. Privileging this kind of "knowledge" is a consequence of the "refugee-trauma" narrative, following the exclusively pathological way that trauma is understood today.

However, if we were to examine more carefully the sequence of the "refugee trauma", we would discern a number of distinct phases that are not all about the devastating events that may have occurred. More specifically, the predominant way of understanding trauma is in a simplistic monocausal way, as if it were a line that divided a person's life into two parts—before and after (see Figure 9.1) the exposure to war atrocities. This way of understanding refugee trauma implies that life before the line was fine and

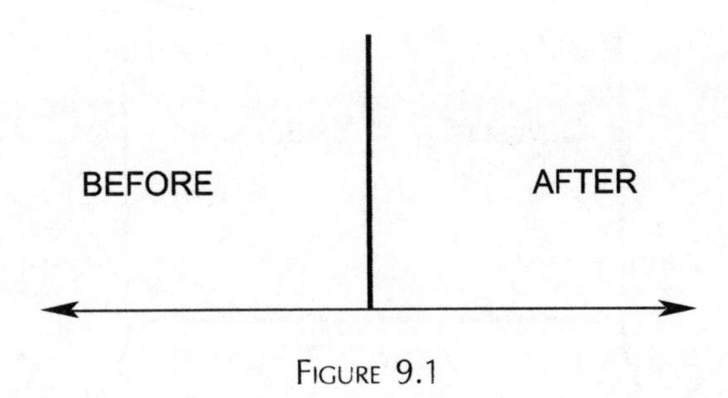

FIGURE 9.1

unproblematic and only the devastating events of the war atrocities count. It is as if only these events could be responsible for producing "the" unique piece of information that would make a difference in understanding a refugee's present predicament. Without denying the reality or the painful impact of such events, it is important to acknowledge that not all refugees have experienced such atrocities. Many hear about the imminent danger and flee in time. Yet it is compelling to comprehend human pain in terms of some concrete evidence that raw violence had occurred, which was the actual source and cause of the refugee's present suffering. This concretization is one of the seeming benefits of the refugee-trauma narrative.

In short, I would argue that the dividing line is not just one point in time but consists of at least two phases. The first is the phase of what could be called Devastating Events, and the second, that of Survival (see Figure 9.2). The first covers the period of war atrocities, for those refugees who experience such events. This phase is followed by the phase of Survival, during which refugees are no longer in physical danger from enemy action. They are safe and protected in sanctioned places, living in tents or in abandoned

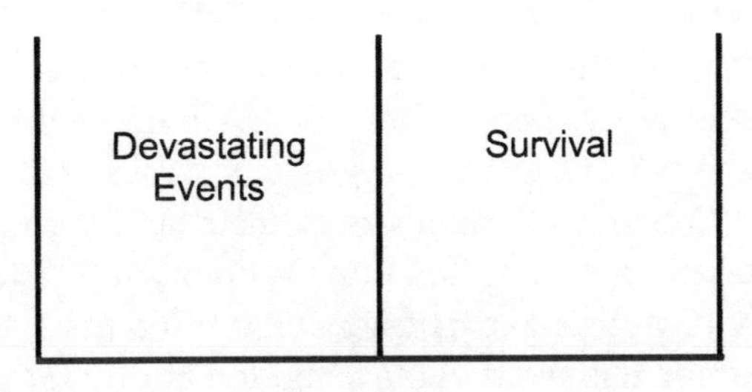

FIGURE 9.2

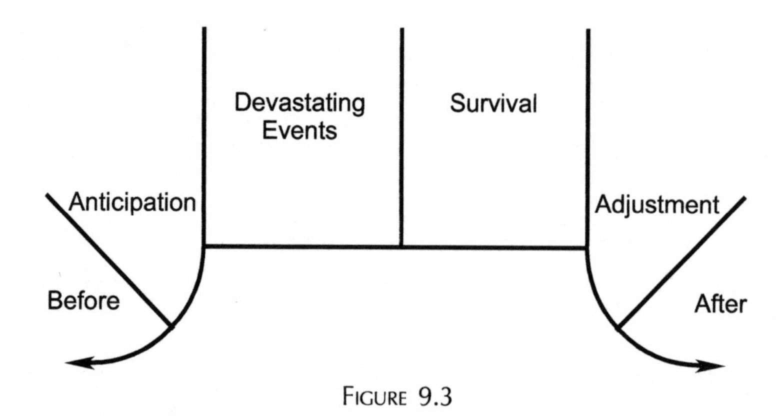

FIGURE 9.3

schools, factories, or other large buildings. However, although their lives are no longer threatened, this does not mean that this phase is free from any intense suffering. On the contrary—during this phase, refugees are disoriented, disempowered, and helpless. They may not know where members of their family are, where they will go, or what will happen to them, and they wait for their fate to be decided by politicians, international organizations, and warlords. They do not follow their usual daily routine and do not perform their usual roles; instead, they sit aimlessly waiting for long and empty periods of time, sometimes even for years, without their usual support systems in their original community. This can be a most distressing and indeed "traumatic" phase, which is usually ignored, especially when the emphasis is on the exciting and tangible Devastating Events phase.

These two phases are not the only ones that constitute refugee trauma. At least two more can be identified: the phases of Anticipation and Adjustment (see Figure 9.3). The phase of Anticipation comes before the Devastating Events phase, in what is usually considered to be the "pre-traumatic period", if trauma is understood to refer exclusively to the Devastating Events. During this phase of uncertainty, people hear of the imminent danger and embark on the painful process of guessing which decision would be the correct one for all members of their family and for everything else taken into consideration. Without solid structures to rely on, they have to make decisions that often mark the fate not only of them but also their whole extended family for generations to come. Should they flee or stay? Should they take all their possessions or just some of them, and which ones? Should they all go together or separate into smaller groups and take different routes? "This is a most 'traumatic' phase because due to the overall chaotic circumstances and the breakdown of positive authority, law and order, there are no guidelines or predictions that apply to such a situation" (Papadopoulos, 2000b). There are many refugees who in many subsequent years suffer more from this phase than from any other. Recriminations, blame of each other, and the agonizing "what if" questions can torment refugees throughout the rest of their lives about the decisions they reached during this phase. Lastly, the phase of Survival is followed by another period, that of Adjustment, which refers to the most difficult time after they arrive in the receiving country to begin their new lives. The expectations and high hopes are often crushed by the harsh reality that is filled by disorientation, helplessness, bitterness, anger, and ambivalence towards the refugee workers and all other agencies that try to help them (Papadopoulos, 1999a). Moreover, conflict and rivalry among aid organizations and services may make them pawns in other battles of a different nature where the rules are less graspable than open warfare.

Refugee-trauma implications

As we have seen, the idea of "refugee trauma" defined in a monocausal way and referring to the phase of Devastating Events can offer a simple, convenient, and discrete way of conceptualizing human suffering under otherwise difficult circumstances. Such a simplified formula can be most consoling in addressing highly complex situations that are not only difficult to grasp intellectually, but also painful emotionally as well as confusing epistemologically. However, the simplification that the "refugee-trauma" discourse offers can do violence to an already multifaceted and multidimensional field such as the refugee situation. Despite the misleading "self-evident" situation, as we have seen, the source or cause of refugee trauma is not just one single and identifiable event. Moreover, our justified abhorrence of the atrocities that are considered the cause of refugee trauma may force us into creating a simplistic causal relation between the atrocities and the "trauma", thus ignoring the possibility of a non-pathological response to the condemnable atrocities. In other words, the epistemological confusion between morality and pathology may lead to uniform pathologization of the refugee situation. All systemic complexities are ignored when we see refugees as simply an indiscriminate group of traumatized individuals.

Other interrelated implications of accepting this widespread and predominant version of the "refugee trauma" discourse include the distance that is created between therapists and the suffering refugees, the fostering of dependence, the diminishment of psychological complexities, the setting up of polarized situations, the creation of victim–saviour dyads, and the denial of resilience and other positive outcomes. Although it is impossible to address all these implications in any detail in the context of this chapter, it will suffice to outline their basic parameters. Most of these implications are interrelated with each other, and the one follows from the other.

With the good intentions of assisting the suffering refugees, once we adopt unquestionably the "refugee-trauma" discourse we are likely to find ourselves entangled in most of these implications. By assuming that the refugee has been inexorably traumatized by war atrocities, we create a barrier between them, their suffering, and us, who have not been exposed to that kind of atrocity; this is a paradoxical mechanism that keeps at bay those people whom we want to assist. If they suffer from something that was caused by a unique historical event that is so foreign to their therapists in the receiving country, then this differentiation creates a gap that is difficult to bridge. In conjunction with the assumption that the refugees are so damaged and their resilience or other positive qualities are not discernible, then inevitably they will need to rely entirely on their therapists' assistance in ways that foster cycles of dependence. Such cycles are difficult to break because the more therapists and other aid workers try to help, the more they tend to locate their client refugees as helpless and dependent persons. Another vicious cycle that is set up by implicitly adopting this version of refugee trauma is the potentially lethal interlocking of victim–saviour positions. If the refugee is seen as just a victim, invariably the position of the saviour is going to be evoked in the therapists. It is fairly impossible to sit in front of victims without feelings of saving them not emerging in the therapist. However, this scenario does not stop here; the dyad of victim–saviour must also produce the position of a perpetrator or violator. Saviours do not save victims without an attempt to protect them from their violators. Although it is appropriate for therapists to reject abstract neutrality and to express their abhorrence against atrocities and to condemn those individuals and groups that have been responsible for such abominable actions, the systemic triangle does not stop there. It is very likely that therapists and refugees, under these conditions, will extend this condemnation against other violators that the system will create. Thus, it is not uncommon for this victim–saviour dyad to keep on producing increasingly more enemies that they will need to defend themselves against, such as the managers of the therapists' services and other individuals and bodies that do not offer the kind of unconditional support that the dyad expects and demands.

The denial of complexity (which the "refugee trauma" promotes) may also deprive therapeutic work in these contexts from accessing the totality of psychological functions and abilities of refugees. Ultimately, human beings have the capacity to process internally and within their families and communities painful events and experiences, and to transform them into potentially growthful potentialities. Therapeutic work that is focused too closely on refugee trauma as a monocausal pathological phenomenon will fail to capitalize on this potential; the positive use of the role of imagination, symbolization, as well as the whole transference countertransference matrix can be underestimated or completely ignored. In systemically informed work with refugees, this potentiality is equally present especially when the systemic interconnections among the various positions in such vicious cycles and the other interrelated dimensions and systems are addressed.

Thus, paradoxically, in working with refugees, by increasing the level of complexity, despite the pressure to keep things "simple", new patterns can emerge that can not only produce epistemological clarity but also free both therapists and refugees from falling into fixed, sterile, and polarized positions.

What knowledge can be supervised, and how?

Zahra's case illustrates the point suggested by the title of this chapter—that is, that therapists and other refugee workers, under the imperceptible influence of the refugee-trauma discourse, tend to feel that they cannot work effectively with this group of clients unless they have some privileged knowledge. From the above discussion, it emerges that they must be referring to two types of knowledge: one is about the details of the war atrocities that it is believed were the cause of the trauma, and the other is specialist knowledge about the intricacies of this unique group of people which therapists believe are going to be indispensable for their work with refugees. It is important for the systemic supervisors to appreciate the genuine nature of this need for both kinds of knowledge; however, at the same time, it is equally important not to attempt to provide this desired knowledge. This need in therapists is a product of an erroneous epistemology that does not indicate a failing or any deficiency in the therapist but is a product of the wider professional and societal narratives about "refugee trauma".

As we have seen, the "refugee-trauma" discourse can create an astonishing blindness to facets of our clinical work that, under other conditions (if they were not referring to the refugee situation), would have been easily identified and appropriately addressed. In this way, working with refugees constitutes specialist work only insofar as it is imperative to disentangle the various interconnected systems so that clinical clarity will emerge. Ultimately, as supervisors in these contexts, our task is to fathom out the way that this work positions us as therapists (Papadopoulos, 1999a) and as supervisors. The trauma discourse, along with the specific multidimensional nature of the refugeedom, creates a certain type of confusion that can easily have a paralytic effect on both therapists and supervisors alike.

Despite the wealth of information about refugees, mental health, and trauma, there is relatively limited literature on therapeutic approaches to this group of people (De Jong & Clarke, 1996; Goderez, 1987; Montgomery, 1998; Scott & Palmer, 1999; Ursano & McCaughey, 1995; Veer, 1994) and even less from a systemic perspective (Kelley, 1994; Papadopoulos, 1999a; Reichelt & Sveaass,

1994; Woodcock, 1994). By and large, the literature on supervision in family therapy does not address directly the above complexities, although there are papers that could be applicable (e.g. Emerson, 1996; Lee, 1999; Rambo & Shilts, 1997; Roberts, Winek, & Mulgrew, 1999; Sprenkle, 1999; Wieling & Marshall, 1999). Some of the ways that I have found useful in eliciting clearer awareness of our "positioning" (cf. Harré & van Langenhove, 1998) and of the effects of the trauma discourse in supervising work with refugees have included inviting the supervisees to do the following:

1. To map out the various agencies involved in the work and then to consider the ways they are interconnected in terms of their remit and main concerns; subsequently, to consider the ways that the supervisees are positioned as a result of these interconnections.
2. To consider how differently the refugee family could have been conceptualized by their service/agency and themselves (supervisees), had they not been refugees.
3. To consider how differently the family would have been conceptualized had the supervisees possessed the two types of the desired knowledge—that is, knowledge about the "causes" of "trauma", and expert knowledge about the "speciality" of refugee work.
4. To reverse the "pathology" model and see the refugee family not (only) as a source of "problems" but as an example of human resilience; more specifically, to identify the various aspects of resilience that they exhibit, as well as what we could learn from them.
5. To consider how similarly or differently other families they work with (who are not refugees) would have reacted had they been refugees.
6. To consider the range of wider discourses that impact on their therapeutic relationship and to identify other concerns in addition to or instead of the pressure for the two kinds of knowledge.

When such a systematic and indeed systemic method of enquiry is applied, all kinds of unexpected results appear. For example, in my supervision of a clinical psychologist who works in a specialist refugee service, I was astonished to see that after going through most of the above steps, what emerged as more pressing was not the concern for the "traumatized" refugees (which was the initial request for supervision) but a confusing paralysis in the service. More specifically, members of this specialist service were angry and confused about their role when the social services department of a coastal town "dumped" the responsibility for refugee families on a couple of estate agents' offices in their own town, whom the refugees tended to use as their main sources of support. The specialist refugee service did not know how to position themselves in relation to this most awkward situation. Eventually, my supervisee identified a central dilemma for her service: either to accept this irregularity and offer support and training to the estate agents or to attempt to break the refugees' dependence on them. In another supervision, of a therapist in a GP practice, it emerged after a systemic enquiry along the lines outlined above that one of the disabling factors for the therapist was the imperceptibly increased pressure to work with more refugees in the practice. The initially inexplicable influx of refugee families in the practice was gradually traced to the over-keenness and kindness of one receptionist in the practice. The changed situation with the new demands was not understood appropriately by all concerned in the practice, who were ambivalent both about the actual new influx of refugees and about the receptionist's benevolent loose appreciation of boundaries.

Ultimately, as Zahra's case has demonstrated, systemic supervision in this field may not be about helping therapists to develop specialist techniques in order to extract information from their refugee clients about the causes of their trauma, nor about acquiring sophisticated forms of expertise in this field. As Bateson (1967) put it, "Evidently, the nature of 'meaning,' pattern, redundancy, information and the like, depends upon where we sit" (p. 407). In this way, systemic supervision with refugees can be effective when we throw some light on where the wider discourses, which mostly appear as background noise, make us sit.

Acknowledgement. I wish to thank Andrea Smollan for allowing me to include her account of my supervision of her work with Zahra. A modified form of this chapter appeared in the *Journal of Family Therapy.*

Comments

The authors of the chapters in this part have highlighted a number of themes related to supervising in very complex contexts. First, there is the importance placed by supervisors on their part in contributing towards the development of a safe context for learning and risk taking. Second, that supervision involves the supervisor owning and sharing her or his knowledge and expertise in a direct way (e.g. "this is what I think") as well as the eliciting of knowledge and expertise from the person supervised. Third, that it is crucial to hold in mind the need to explore matters relating to the professional network. Fourth—and perhaps this is an increasingly vital issue in a multicultural society—that the sociopolitical-cultural context needs to be considered as part of, and not marginal to, supervision and therapy processes. Last, there is the recognition of the importance of encouraging supervisee self-reflexivity, a task of supervision that would hardly have been acknowledged as such ten years ago.

PART IV

A PERSPECTIVE ON EVALUATION

CHAPTER 10

Supervision and clinical governance

Margaret Bennett, Myrna Gower,
Cynthia Maynerd, & Gill Wyse

Supervision is a multi-layered process involving multiple systems and subsystems. Clinical supervision offers many stimulating opportunities and magical moments related to families' progress and trainees' development. It can also be an isolating role in relation to one's peers. Multiple demands and priorities often result in limited opportunity outside individual supervision to develop practice, widen the supervisory repertoire, or avail oneself of what Bateson described as news of a *difference* (Bateson, 1972). Often the time a supervisor would ideally allocate for this purpose becomes constrained as other responsibilities are privileged.

In this chapter we explore our journey into seeking *difference* by using recursive and reflective processes. Our beliefs about the use of a reflecting process in our supervision have been guided by several ideas. Andersen (1993) speaks of the reflecting process, as "open talks". We have adopted a practice that moves towards this objective, following the criteria presented by Andersen for using a reflecting team. We are therefore affirming of each other's practice while contextualizing comments that may be curious, or questioning. We believe it is useful to have multiple descriptions, which are non-judgemental, non-pejorative, and non-directive, as in this way we create a context for change for each other and can begin a journey onwards from the "comfort of the known" to the "excitement and the anxiety of change".

The portion of time that supervisors spend focusing on development seems similar to the portion of food that the parent in a large family gives her/himself when a moderate amount has to go a long way. This can result in a familiar and ongoing pattern. We have attempted to address this small portion in our institution, in a way that is isomorphic with the needs of trainees and families, by developing collaboratively a practice of "supervision of supervisors".

As a group of four supervisors, we were excited by the timely announcement of the joint Institute of Family Therapy and Tavistock Clinic conference on supervision in 1999. We welcomed the opportunity of presenting to peers the model of supervision we were developing. The conference provided an opportunity for the further development and sharing of ideas. Like de Shazer's notion of pre-session change (Weiner-Davis, de Shazer, & Gingerich, 1987), preparation for presentation at the conference prompted us to consider what changes were occurring in the wider context that might be influencing our future practice. We thought especially about the wider system that contextualized the teaching clinic we supervised in, the changes in the delivery of health care, and the refocusing on notions of accountability.

Our intention of presenting our ideas at a workshop at the conference was to extend the discussion and debate about the development of a supervisory audit and consider how this process could be further enhanced. We asked the members of the workshop to assume the position of professionals in the wider NHS system (e.g. NHS manager, clinical governance co-ordinator, researcher) and also that of a family member and then reflect back to us their ideas about the efficacy of our supervisory audit model. This resonated with our theme of contextualizing our practice and responding to the requirements of clinical audit.

It was valuable to us to have had the experience of exposing our ideas and therapeutic practice to the comments of experienced colleagues in the workshop. It was important to have a multiplicity of views and to be connected with a wider group of supervisors in order to expand our horizons. (This workshop has now been presented to a further wide audience at the International Family Therapy Association conference in Oslo in June 2000.)

We also asked the participants to evaluate the whole workshop, remembering again the value of Andersen's "outer talks" (1993). As well as valuing the ideas of systemic colleagues in the workshop, we also tried to create a context whereby we could "hear" the voices of the wider health system—that is, those of colleagues and client families who would not be likely to focus on systemic concepts. The ideas we presented regarding our supervisory role are consistent with and mirror our views about the ethics that inform our practice as therapists. In both situations, there is respect and value for differing points of view and different contexts.

The clinic where we work is located in a community with a multicultural population. The trainees and client families come from diverse backgrounds and ages. We are a group of white women in mid-life, and so we value opportunities such as the 1999 conference to check with other professionals ideas with respect to gender, age, and ethnic diversity.

In 1997, the U.K. government announced a plan for modernizing the health service. The linchpin of this proposal is clinical governance, which directs professionals to develop ways of auditing clinical practice. We thought it relevant to begin the chapter with a brief description of clinical governance and the place of clinical audit. We then describe the context in which our supervision occurs—the development of supervision of supervisors—and present feedback from various positions in the supervisory system.

The New NHS

In a white paper, *The New NHS: Modern and Dependable* (Department of Health, 1997) and the consultation document, *A First Class Service* (Department of Health, 1998), the government set out a ten-year plan to build a modern and dependable health service with fair access and quality care for all patients. The main components of the plan are:

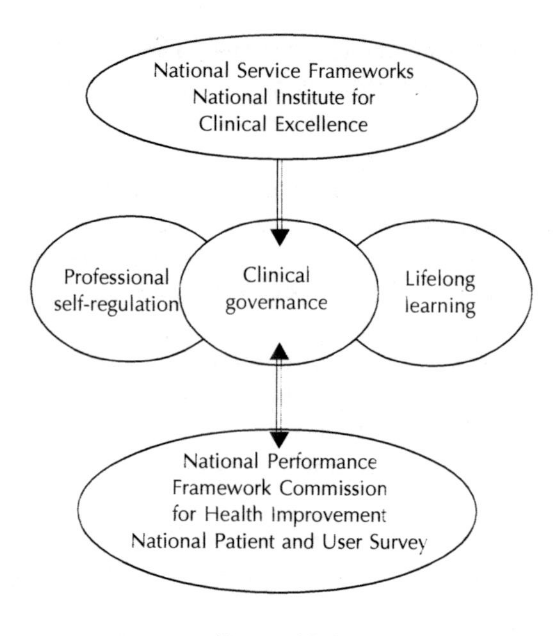

FIGURE 10.1

- clear national standards for services and treatment
- local delivery of high quality healthcare
- effective systems for monitoring the delivery of quality standards

The new system as visualized in the proposals is shown in Figure 10.1. The circularity and interconnectedness of various parts of the system are highlighted, with clinical governance as the central focus.

Clinical governance

Clinical governance is presented as a framework through which organizations in the NHS are accountable for continuously reviewing and improving the quality of services. It places expectations and responsibilities on individuals and organizations to develop systems to ensure the delivery of high-quality care. There are requirements that professionals within the NHS have clear policies aimed at managing risk and procedures for identifying and managing poor performance.

Professional self-regulation

Through their professional body, the Association for Family Therapy and Systemic Practice, family therapists have in place structures for training and registering family therapists and new procedures for registering supervisors. These structures would be complementary to developing systems of monitoring and appraising professional performance within the NHS.

Clinical audit

One of the key dimensions of clinical governance is clinical audit. Family therapists will be required to assess the service they give in relation to established standards. Clinical audit is a process for ensuring quality service by reviewing practice, drawing conclusions, and recommending and implementing changes. The initial step is often meeting the challenge of developing and setting standards. The model of "supervision of supervision" that we describe here could contribute to this process in relation to auditing supervision.

As circularity is a core feature of systemic thinking, clinical audit is a concept that systemic thinkers are well equipped to manage. Family therapists have begun to share their experiences of clinical audit in a variety of settings (e.g. Blumenthal, Seth, Turnbull, Mouratoglou, & David, 1998).

In the *Focus* publication on clinical audit in child and adolescent psychiatry (Royal College of Psychiatrists, 1998), the cyclical aspect of audit is highlighted. In practice this means that for the audit loop to be closed, changes in practice should be made and then re-audited regarding implementation and effectiveness. While developing standards in family therapy practice, we have all become used to changing practice in demonstrable ways—for example, by obtaining feedback from participants and implementing changes as a result.

Continuing professional development

Within the governmental guidance, it is recognized that clinical governance needs to be underpinned by an open and participative blame-free culture that values peer review and promotes what is called lifelong learning. This is familiar territory for family therapists. The main challenges in respect of supervision will be to construct standards collaboratively so those supervisors in different parts of the country do not find themselves reinventing the proverbial wheel.

In summary, in the health trust in which we work we believe that there are several ways in which supervisors will be required to contribute to the development of clinical governance:

- developing standards of clinical practice
- promoting professional self-regulation
- supporting audit and relating it to learning needs
- promoting lifelong learning.

For supervisors, these proposals will require a strategic fit between a systemic position that promotes reflection and curiosity and an organizational strategy that names excellence and efficiency as its goals. The context for the development of this plan will be within organizations where financial constraints are a reality. Supervisors are frequently also confronting these realities, with trainees trying to obtain funding and families in deprived social circumstances. However, family therapists have always been good at pioneering in adverse circumstances, and, despite the many constraints, we have enjoyed developing our work together.

How it all began—supervision of supervisors

The seeds of the idea of annual live supervision of supervisors that we have now established at the Prudence Skynner Family Therapy Clinic arose out of a staff meeting in 1993. We commenced the process in 1994.

The context

The Prudence Skynner Family Therapy Clinic was originally developed within the psychotherapy department of St. George's Hospital, London, and moved to its present site in the grounds of Springfield Psychiatric Hospital in the late 1970s.

The clinic was formally opened in 1989 by Dr. Robin Skynner (pioneer of family therapy in the U.K., who died in the summer of 2000) and named after his late wife, Prudence. The training course is unique within the U.K. in being based within adult mental health services. A clinical diploma course was first offered in 1988.

Currently the clinic offers a range of training courses and services, from foundation level to qualifying level. The Association of Family Therapy accredits the courses.

The services currently provided include specialist clinics for:

- the elderly and their families
- families in which one member has a learning disability
- families in which one member is deaf
- families in which one member has a psychotic illness (the newest clinic)
- short-term experience of systemic work to specialist/senior registrars
- some families from the children's eating-disorder service.

There are also four clinics for the training teams, each with a supervisor.

The qualifying diploma course

Since the clinics' inception, there have been 102 trainees, of whom 77 have achieved a Diploma. The trainees have been drawn from diverse professional backgrounds, as indicated in Table 10.1.

The diploma course is arranged for two days per week and lasts for two academic years. There is an intake each year, so one of the days is for the first-year trainee supervision group and the other for

TABLE 10.1

Professional Background	*Number of Trainees*
Nurses	46
Social workers	24
Counsellors	10
Psychiatrists/paediatricians/ general practitioners	9
Psychologists	8
Occupational therapists	3
Probation officers	2

the second-year trainee supervision group. The average number of trainees in each team is four.

We have been fortunate for the last ten years to have had the same director in post, Barbara Warner. As course director, Barbara has had a busy role both teaching on and running the course. The supervisors are responsible for the supervision of the therapeutic work of the team, the integration of theoretical knowledge and clinical practice; contributing to the teaching of study days, co-marking the termly essays with the course director, and contributing to the final evaluation process.

The supervisors have some common forums: namely, termly supervisors' meetings, joint teaching, and joint presentations at conferences and workshops. They are responsible, together with the course director, for the overall clinical assessment of the trainees.

Since 1993, a foundation-level course has been taught annually by two of the supervisors. This has become one of the main sources of applicants to the diploma course. There have been 98 participants on this course.

In 1993, a clinical practicum was also established. Its purpose is to provide a forum for the diploma holders to continue to deepen and broaden their theoretical knowledge and clinical skills. Two of the supervisors have been involved in supervising this course.

The evolution of the supervisor "audit" process

At the staff meeting in 1993, the context for the discussion was the Prudence Skynner supervisors' concern to develop their supervisory skills to maintain their high standards of supervision and keep themselves focused on the process. We wanted evidence for what we did well and a method of demonstrating where there was scope for improvement. At this stage in 1993, "clinical governance" was not part of everyday health-trust vocabulary! Nevertheless, we were concerned to prioritize continually developing our standards. What we initially called "supervisors' supervision" has evolved over time to include the wider context and changing patterns in our professional training standards and organizational requirements. We describe in this section our developing process and then seek to link it with the current focus on clinical audit.

Our existing written evaluation document for the trainees allowed for their input into how relevant the supervisory process was to them as individuals. What we needed was to utilize the experience and skills of the individual members of the supervisory team to focus on the process.

We integrated ideas of a "supervision training" model that had been developed in supervisor evaluation in social work training. One of our number had being doing some work as a trainer for experienced social workers, who were themselves training to become teachers of social work. One of her roles was to live-supervise the trainee teacher when she was supervising her social work student. The trainee teachers had, by definition, to have been qualified and practising as social workers for some time before they could take on the additional responsibility and become part of the university practice-teachers' course. There were two issues arising from the supervision of the trainee teachers which were important to us in the audit of our own supervision: first, the anxiety felt by experienced practitioners when being observed in a teaching/supervisory context, even though they themselves were skilled experienced professionals; second, the universal reports of the usefulness of the experience, to the practice teachers, which permeated into other aspects of their professional life.

One of the reflections we wanted to bring into our family therapy supervision audit was to reintroduce ourselves to the adrenaline rush of feeling, anxiety, excitement, and sharp focus that working under supervision often brings.

In planning the supervision we were anxious not to de-skill the trainee family therapists, who might be unused to live supervision. Like all systemic trainers, we are familiar with the comments from experienced senior doctors, psychologists, social workers, and nurses on how de-skilled they feel as they struggle in front of a one-way screen for the first time while learning to be systemic therapists. The first time we supervised the family therapy trainee, with our colleagues observing and supervising our supervision, our minds were wonderfully concentrated on the effects and processes of feeling de-skilled. Nevertheless, it seemed properly ethical to demonstrate to the trainees that it was appropriate to put ourselves within a similar process in our goal of improving practice and delivering high standards of training. We reflected again on Andersen's notions of reflexivity (1993) being non-pejorative and "outer talks" contextualized.

The model: the development of multilayered supervision

We decided to begin this "supervising the supervisors" process with a second-year group of supervision trainees rather than a first-year group, who might not feel as confident. It was initially anticipated that each training cohort would therefore initially undergo the experience once in his or her training. Later on, we would develop this to be an annual event for each trainee group and supervisor, as it would be important to audit supervision at all stages of the therapist's training.

In conjunction with the trainees, we developed a model of three supervisors live-supervising one family therapist supervisor with her team for one whole session (see Figure 10.2). The three visiting supervisors observed the pre-session discussion, the therapeutic session, and the post-session discussion. With two teams this took a morning. We then designed the afternoon to be a combination of live feedback on the supervisory process to each of the two supervisors for that day and reflections from the trainees on being an actual therapist within this process, as well as being a

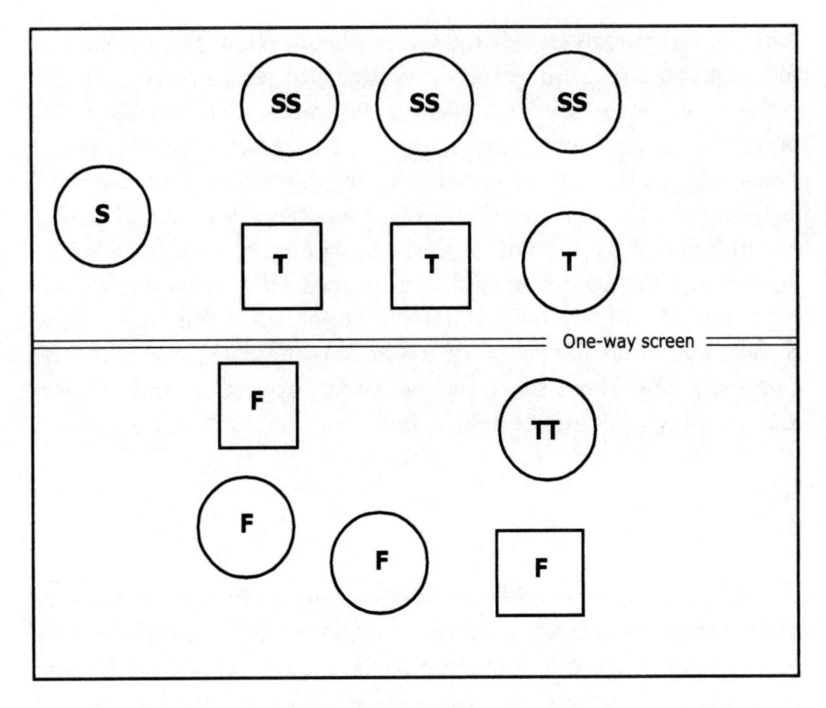

FIGURE 10.2
(SS = supervising supervisor; S = supervisor; T = trainee; TT = trainee therapist; F = family member)

team member and being part of the process for their training team. The supervisors also reflected on the process of learning about their supervision: what they had gained from it, how they had felt, what had been difficult, and what had been helpful.

So far we have not involved the families' reflections beyond seeking their agreement to the three supervisors being present in their therapy session; we give the families a careful explanation about our purpose and our process and our focus on professional standards. We also offer to introduce them to the three supervisors who are behind the screen while their family's concerns are being dealt with by the trainee family therapist and team.

In our preliminary discussions before we had inaugurated the supervisory audit process, we had hypothesized about possible worries for ourselves. All four supervisors come from a similar professional background (social work), and we have been in the supervisory team for some years. We value each other's skills, perspectives, and observations—although we by no means always agree with each other: together with the course director, we have had some lively staff meetings! What we had not anticipated was our individual anxiety within the new experience and the *frisson* of doubt and mistrust that suddenly appeared in relation to our colleagues. Self-justifying comments appeared at the edge of our conversations. In the midst of the adrenaline rush, one could be aware of new communication between supervisor and trainee, and the new dialogue emerging between one's colleagues.

Teaching contexts

When in a teaching context and developing further understanding of the model as happened at the joint conference in 1999, we have found it helpful to ask workshop participants to take part in some experiential exercises to enable them to reflect further on the model.

What we seek to raise in the execution of the exercises is to make available for discussion the different dilemmas raised from different points in the system when a group of colleagues engage in mutual supervision of supervision. This further explores some of our ideas about the process and helps to clarify various aspects of our thinking—for example, paying attention to the significant views of the wider system, including management.

Ideological differences

At times we have to supervise practice where the supervisee's ideas are based on opposite or certainly different premises from those of our own. We are aware that ways of supervising often differ from the ideology of the clinical practice being taught—for example, supervising structural or strategic skills within a supervisory frame where ideological differences of hierarchy exist can prove confusing. We are not permitted exclusive specialisms, since as supervisors we have to be open to as many ideas as possible if we are to be collaborative and earn the regard of our colleague. From the position of the "observing supervisor", what becomes evident is that what is sought is not "the right practice" but, rather, different practices. We are both trainees and teachers, at all times seeking new techniques if we want to stay in line with current developments in practice. As supervisors, we are always trying to catch up with new ideas in the clinical field, let alone teaching methods. Often we have to unlearn so much of what we have held dear in our own learning.

Our curiosity as observing colleagues needed, importantly, to stem from a position of relevant curiosity rather than vicarious curiosity if learning was to take place. This, as mentioned earlier, presumed considerable trust between colleagues.

Definition of responsibility

Levels of responsibility and therefore levels of influence were defined from each point in the system during the exercise. It was at the workshop that we emphasized the importance of different people's participation and extended the exercise as more than simply a developmental task for the supervisors, as initially construed. The complexity of the event emerged and, in discussion, almost seemed as if its repetition could be contraindicated in the face of overwhelming organizational resistance. It reminded us of those role-plays that we had experienced in training new systemic therapists where the role-playing family presented so many difficulties for the trainee therapist that the trainee either had to be rescued or "threw in the towel".

Responsibility in both therapy and supervision must be well defined for the good outcome of the process. It is important to agree how, in each role, one wants to deploy one's influence. The observing supervisor needs to remain responsible "for the supervision of supervision", while the supervisor of the team remains clinically responsible for the successful outcome of work with the family.

Of particular importance is the acknowledgement that the supervision of colleagues' supervision is a mutual evaluation of performance. For the task to prove useful, the lines of responsibility need to be clear, as, organizationally, there may be insufficient boundaries to permit observation and open learning. The supervisors need to prepare well for the task beforehand to ensure such clarity. The supervisors needed to have clear and realistic objectives and to be prepared to share feedback with the full group.

Trainees' views of the supervision

Although the purpose of the exercise was primarily to enable the supervisors to receive mutual feedback and reflect on their own supervisory process, it was important that the trainees were also invited to respond with their reactions to the experience.

For use in training workshops, we have videoed three trainees describing, to their supervisors, the impact of the exercise upon them and their views about it. For the purposes of this chapter, two transcripts have been used.

Trainee A

How do you remember the day?

"I remember being behind the screen with two extra people I hadn't met before. It was different. I think that meant the team discussion wasn't what it used to be."

What did you understand was the purpose of the day?

"I understood they [the visiting supervisors] were assessing our supervisor, that it was a sort of appraisal and we [the trainees] were there to help in that process."

What did you think was the impact of the exercise on the supervisor?

"I remember that there was more anxiety around. It seemed to me to be a slightly artificial set-up because there were three extra people and they weren't contributing to the discussion. I found that inhibiting. They were there but not taking part in the discussion."

Do you think the supervision was any different on that day? In what way might it have been?

"I think the supervisor was more anxious. I don't remember it being different in terms of quality. I think the supervisor might have intervened more than on other occasions. My main memory as a member of the team was of it being slightly uncomfortable. I wondered what the two observers were thinking about the whole thing. For me personally, it changed the focus of what I was thinking about.

Having been part of such an experience, do you have any ideas about how this model might be developed further?

"It's always difficult if people are introduced into a team in which they don't take part in the discussion. I wonder if it would make them less able to assess what the supervisor was doing if they joined in the discussion? I can understand why they wouldn't want to do that, because they wouldn't want to change the supervision in any sense, but by being there they were changing it. We were all probably reacting differently from how we normally were. I think it was quite reassuring for me, as a trainee, to know that this was part of the management of the course. It was good that the supervisors were looking at each other's work and keeping an eye on each other's practice. It made me think that they took the quality of the supervision very seriously. It was obviously important. I suppose the fact that the supervisors were able to do that for each other and accept feedback from each other was important as a model of how we might be as trainee therapists."

TRAINEE B

What understanding did you have of the purpose of the exercise?

"I think we understood clearly what it was for and that supervisors from the opposite year group would come and sit in while you were supervising members of your own team, and that afterwards there would be a joint meeting between the two teams and the supervisors, with feedback to yourself, and there would be a sort of open forum for comments to be made about how that experienced person felt to everyone involved."

Did you have a sense of a position of influence in relation to the supervisory process?

"I can see now that it could be, but at the time I didn't feel it as an influential position. I was aware that we had been invited to make any comments we felt were relevant, or about something that caught our attention, but I didn't see that at that time as being influential in any way."

What did you think might be the impact of this day for the supervisors?

"I and the other team members were quite aware that it was anxiety provoking for you, even on the run up to the day, not just necessarily on the day. We had had previous discussions about it. There was a feeling that you laid bare your practice for other people to look at in terms of responsibility for students. I think the only other thing is that I think it creates anxiety for whoever the therapist is as well."

And on the day you were the therapist. Was the supervision on the day any different from on any other day that we had worked together—do you recall?

"Very probably. I think that you said to me that you would try to keep it as normal as possible. I don't remember feeling more stressed or more aware of you phoning in, or having contact with me more than you would at any other time. I think the anxiety you have with this is that you have then got three extra trained supervisors behind the screen and although they are ostensibly there to supervise your [supervisor] practice, they will also be watching my session, and I think, as a therapist, you feel a loyalty to perhaps trying to give a good session for your supervisor on that day—not that you wouldn't give a good session anyway, but . . ."

Could you give some idea of the flavour of the conversation with your fellow trainees when you had lunch together in the middle of the day?

"I think some people were more vocal about it than others—but that is always the way with groups. I think there was a feeling between the two teams of students that we were obviously aware that our two individual supervisors had very different styles. We wondered how the supervisors who had come in to supervise you were going to keep systemic in their comments about how you actually supervised your teams of students, given the very different styles, and hoped that it wouldn't turn into a sort of divide between two different styles and whether one was good or bad. I don't think that happened in the meeting that we had."

Could you think about dilemmas that were raised?

"I am not saying we didn't say anything, but I think people were probably conservative in their comments. In my view, you are reticent to . . . I think as a student you have a loyalty to your supervisor not because the supervisor is not good—I am not saying that, and there is a loyalty there. The other team, I think, would have felt the same. The supervisors, who came in to supervise you, you all know each other. You all know each other's practice, and there is a familiarity between you. How do you actually have reliable consultation? It is more difficult, I think, sometimes to be in a position where you know people to pass comment on their practice, and that was what the students felt at the time. Did that create difficulties considering that you all knew each other? If you actually felt a supervisor had made a real mistake or a real piece of malpractice, how would you deal with this, if that eventuality did occur?"

Would you comment if you found the exercise reassuring at any level?

"I think there are probably two things to say. I think, as a student, particularly in your early days, you know your supervisors are the fount of all knowledge, so you don't actually see them as laying themselves open because you hold them in that position. But, saying that, I think in our team, particularly with you, we were very aware that you felt that you were laying yourself open, not to criticism but to new points on how you managed your team and your students, and it was reassuring to know that you were prepared to put yourself in that position and to be accountable really for your practice. So yes, it was reassuring."

Do you think it made any difference to our working as a group?

"In our team? I don't think it actually altered how you supervised us from then on in. As a student, I didn't feel a sense that you supervised us in a different manner. It doesn't mean to say you haven't taken note of what was said."

Are there any other comments or suggestions you might make for the future of such an exercise—would you recommend it?

"From the position of a trainee, I think it should be done. Although I spoke about the anxiety, it is not so much that you couldn't cope with it, or not bear with it. But I think it probably was useful. It was useful, I think, for the two teams to meet afterwards because there was discussion about the different styles of supervision, and it was useful because the students—it is quite interesting—are in your team and you don't actually have any other experience of anything else. It was useful to have that sort of forum where you heard of a different type of experience that was as meaningful as your own."

Do you think that the supervision should be audited?

"Yes."

Evaluation

In aiming to be coherent with our style of supervision and our beliefs in the value of co-constructed learning, we also invited the workshop participants to provide us with a written evaluation of the workshop, and we will take these comments forward into our developing process.

CONCLUSION: REFLEXIVITY

Haley (1996) tells us that the goal of supervision is to produce therapists who improve upon what they learn. The mutuality of this task is to supervise colleagues in a way that sharing experiences ensures that each improves upon what they experience both as observers of the supervisors and from feedback of being observed. The two trainee experiences outlined above embrace the notions with which we grappled in the execution of the audit process. The value of the challenge to the learning process can be enhanced by the interface of anxiety and excitement in the learning process—a social constructionist position in the belief that knowledge is a co-operative exercise.

In the first transcript, Trainee A commented that the supervisors' presence "changed the focus of what I was thinking about".

Trainee B queried in the second transcript the notion of "how . . . you actually have reliable consultation" when you are familiar with your colleagues' practice. She makes further significant comments about trainees' possible beliefs about the supervisor being the *"fount of knowledge"*.

Trainee B also reflected that the supervisors' acceptance of feedback from each other "was important as a model of how we might be as trainee therapists".

All these conversations prompted further "inner and outer conversations" (Andersen, 1993) for the supervisors.

We can accept that just as problems of the trainee are resolved by changes in relation to supervision, so too are the supervisors' dilemmas confronted and resolved in relation to supervision of supervision. Laura Fruggeri told us at the joint 1999 Institute of Family Therapy/Tavistock Clinic conference that a key dilemma for her in offering consultation is the question: "How can we help people to change without entering the dichotomy that change implies that what went before was wrong?" What she aimed for was a coexistence of perspective. We share this view, since as supervisors we believe that we came to this exercise with a mutual desire to develop our supervisory practice, which we believe, as Fruggeri stated, was supervisors having done "a good job" rather than from a position of supervisory insufficiency. Family therapists no longer take the position referred to by Bryan Lask (1998) when Salvador Minuchin supervised him in 1980: "We would show him a videotape of our work and he would show us the error of our ways."

Even in the face of the many potential organizational complexities, we unanimously agree that the learning and the resulting accountability are worthwhile. We believed others might obtain value from hearing our story. The joint 1999 Institute of Family Therapy/Tavistock Clinic conference and other teaching experiences offer us the opportunity to further develop and reflect on our "Supervisory Audit Ideas" and experience. We will no doubt risk levels of transparency in our practice that we believe we should expect from those whom we teach and to whom we consult. We look forward to the developing process of clinical governance.

We apply some of Gergen's (1985) thoughts to this process. The goal of supervision could accordingly be to participate in a conversation that continually loosens and opens up, rather than constricts and closes down. Through supervisory conversation, fixed meanings and behaviours are given room, broadened, shifted, and changed.

Acknowledgements. We wish to record our appreciation for the help given to us by our three ex-trainee colleagues: Linda Finn, Wendy Gardner, and Linda Jacobs.

Comments

Clinicians are expected to be accountable for the quality of their work, and agency responsibility in the U.K. for clinical work is established through clinical governance. This chapter is an important contribution to that process. This group of family therapists have found a way to evaluate their own supervision through feedback from trainees and, at the same time, contribute to the agency's responsibility to govern or manage clinical work by passing feedback on to management. The authors have opened a debate that most of us are facing, or soon will face, about linking our work as supervisors to the process of clinical governance.

REFERENCES

Andersen, T. (1987). The reflecting team: dialogue and metadialogue in clinical work. *Family Process, 26*: 415–428.

Andersen, T. (Ed.) (1990). *The Reflecting Team: Dialogues and Dialogues about the Dialogues*. Broadstairs: Borgman.

Andersen, T. (1993). See and hear and be seen and heard. In: S. Friedman (Ed.), *The New Language of Change: Constructive Collaboration in Psychotherapy*. New York: Guilford Press.

Andersen, T. (1994). *Reflekterende Processer*. København: Dansk Psykologisk Forlag.

Anderson, H. (1997). *Conversation, Language and Possibilities*. New York: Basic Books.

Anderson, H., & Goolishian, H. (1988). Human systems as linguistic systems: preliminary and evolving ideas about the implications for clinical theory. *Family Process, 27* (4): 371–393.

Anderson, H., & Goolishian, H. (1992b). Therapeutic process as social construction. In: S. McNamee & K. Gergen (Eds.), *Therapy as Social Construction*. London: Sage.

Anderson, H., & Swim, S. (1993). Learning as collaborative conversation. *Human Systems, 4*: 145–153.

Arroyo, W., & Eth, S. (1996). Post-traumatic stress disorder and other stress reactions. In: R. J. Apfel & B. Simon (Eds.), *Minefields in Their*

Hearts: Mental Health of Children in War and Communal Violence (pp. 52–74). New Haven, CT: Yale University Press.

Association for Family Therapy (1995). Ethnicity, culture, race and family therapy. *Context* (Special Edition).

Association for Family Therapy (2000). Spirituality, religion and therapy, *Context, 48* (Special Edition, April).

Bateson, G. (1967). Cybernetic explanation. In: *Steps to an Ecology of Mind*. New York: Ballantine, 1972.

Bateson, G. (1971). The cybernetics of "Self": a theory of alcoholism. In: *Steps to an Ecology of Mind*. New York: Ballantine, 1972.

Bateson, G. (1972). *Steps to an Ecology of Mind*. New York: Ballantine; London: Paladin, 1973.

Bateson, G. (1978). The birth of a matrix or double bind and epistemology. In: M. M. Berger (Ed.), *Beyond the Double Bind* (pp. 39–64). New York: Brunner & Mazel.

Bateson, G., & Bateson, M. C. (1987). *Angels Fear: Toward an Epistemology of the Sacred*. New York: Macmillan.

Bentovim, A. (1992). *Trauma-Organized Systems*. London: Karnac.

Black, R., & Koser, K. (Eds.) (1999). *The End of the Refugee Cycle? Refugee Repatriation and Reconstruction*. New York: Berghahn Books.

Bluementhal, S., Seth, R., Turnbull, G., Mouratoglou, V., & David, A. (1998). Audit of a family therapy clinic in a general hospital setting. *Context, 38*: 32–35.

Börjeson, B., & Håkansson, H. (1998). *Truede børn; socialt arbejde ved anbringelse af børn udenfor hjemmet*, København: Socialpædagogisk bibliotek.

Boscolo, L., Cecchin, G., Hoffman, L., & Penn, P. (1987). *Milan systemic family therapy*. New York: Basic Books.

Bracken, P. J., & Petty, C. (Eds.) (1998). *Rethinking the Trauma of War*. London: Free Association Books.

Brookfield, S. (1995). Adult learning: an overview. In: A. Tuinjman (Ed.), *International Encyclopedia of Education*. Oxford: Pergamon Press.

Bruner, J. (1986). *Actual Minds, Possible Worlds*. Cambridge, MA: Harvard University Press.

Burck, C., & Daniel, G. (1995). Training and supervision: addressing the context of gender. In: *Gender and Family Therapy* (pp. 119–127). London: Karnac.

Burnham, J. (1992). Approach—method—technique: making distinctions and creating connections. *Human Systems, 3* (1): 3–26.

Burnham, J. (1993). Systemic supervision: the evolution of reflexivity in the context of the supervisory relationship. *Human Systems, 4* (Special Issue, 3 & 4): 349–381.

Burnham, J. (2000). Internalised other interviewing: evaluating and enhancing empathy. *Clinical Psychology Forum, 140*: 16–20.

Burnham, J., Daniel, G., Draper, R., & Mason, B. (1996). *The Red Book: Registration of Supervisors and Accreditation of Training Courses: Criteria and Guidelines*. Canterbury: AFT Publishing.

Burnham, J., & Harris, Q. (1996). Emerging ethnicity: a tale of three cultures. In: K. N. Dwivedi & V. P. Varma (Eds.), *Meeting the Needs of Ethnic Minority Children*. London: Jessica Kingsley.

Byng-Hall, J. (1995). *Rewriting Family Scripts*. London: Guilford.

Byng-Hall, J., & Whiffen, R. (1982). Evolution of supervision: an overview. In: *Family Therapy Supervision—Recent Developments in Practice*. London: Academic Press.

Campbell, D., Draper, R., & Huffington, C. (1988). *Teaching Systemic Thinking*. Hampshire: DC Associates.

Capra, F. (1982). *The Turning Point*. New York: Bantam.

Carlier, J.-Y., & Vanheule, D. (Eds.) (1997). *Europe and Refugees: A Challenge?* The Hague: Kluwer.

Carter, B., & McGoldrick, M. (Eds.) (1989). *The Changing Family Life Cycle: A Framework Therapy* (2nd edition). London: Allyn & Bacon.

Caruth, C. (1996). *Unclaimed Experience: Trauma, Narrative and History*. Baltimore, MD: Johns Hopkins University Press.

Cecchin, G. (1987). Hypothesizing, circularity and neutrality, revisited: an invitation to curiosity. *Family Process, 26*: 405–413.

Cecchin, G., Lane, G., & Ray, W. (1994). *The Cybernetics of Prejudices in the Practice of Psychotherapy*. London: Karnac.

Chogyam, N., & Dechen, K. (1997). *Spectrum of Ecstasy: Embracing Emotions as the Path of Inner Tantra*. London : Aro Books.

Cingolani, S. (1995). Come compromettere il bene alla ricerca del meglio. Appunti sulla patologia iatrogena ed i suoi rimedi da un punto di vista relazionale-sistemico. In: M. Bianciardi & U. Telfener (Eds.), *Ammalarsi di psicoterapia* (pp. 115–128). Milan: Angeli.

Clifton, D., et al. (1990). The reauthoring of therapist's stories: taking doses of our own medicine. *Journal of Strategic and Systemic Therapies, 9* (4): 61–66.

CONFETTI (1999). Sowing the seeds of cultural competence: family therapy training for a multi-ethnic society. A report of the CONFETTI working party on "Race Ethnicity and Culture in Family Therapy Training". *Context, 44* (Special Issue, August).

Coupland, N., & Nussbaum, J. (1993). *Discourse and Lifespan Identity.* New York: Sage.

Cronen, V. E., & Pearce, W. B. (1985). Toward an explanation of how the Milan method works: an invitation to a systemic epistemology and the evolution of family systems. In: D. Campbell & R. Draper (Eds.), *Applications of Systemic Therapy: The Milan Approach*. London & New York: Grune & Stratton.

Cutteridge, S. (1992). "Therapist Ethnicity." Unpublished proceedings of course seminars, KCC Diploma in Systemic Therapy.

Dare, C., Eisler, I., Colahan, M., Crowther, C., Senior, R., & Asen, E. (1995). The listening heart and the chi-square: clinical and empirical perceptions in the family therapy of anorexia nervosa. *Journal of Family Therapy, 17* (1).

De Bernart, R., & Dobrowolski, C. (1996). La supervisione clinica nel training. *Terapia Familiare, 52*: 93–106.

De Bono, E. (1993). *Water Logic.* New York: Penguin.

De Jong, J., & Clarke, L. (Eds.) (1996). *Mental Health of Refugees.* Geneva: World Health Organisation/UNHCR.

Department of Health (1997). *The New NHS, Modern and Dependable.* London: HMSO.

Department of Health (1998). *A First Class Service—Quality in the New NHS*. London: HMSO.

Department of Health (1999). *Clinical Governance: Quality in the New NHS*. London: HMSO.

Down, G. (2000). Supervision in a multicultural context. In: G. G. Barnes, G. Down, & D. McCann (Eds.), *Systemic Supervision: A Portable Guide for Supervision Training*. London: Jessica Kingsley.

Draper, R., & Hills, J. (1992). The consulting partnership. *Context, 12*: 29–30.

Egelund, T. (1997). *Beskyttelse af barndommen. Socialforvaltningers risikovurdering og indgreb*. København: Hans Reitzel.

Eisenbruch, M. (1991). From post-traumatic stress disorder to cultural bereavement: diagnosis of Southeast Asian refugees. *Social Sciences and Medicine, 33*: 673–680.

Emerson, S. (1996). Creating a safe place for growth in supervision *Contemporary Family Therapy, 18* (3): 393–404.

Epston, D. (1993). Internalised other interviewing with couple: The New Zealand Version. In: S. Gilligan & P. Reese (Eds.), *Therapeutic Conversations*. New York: Norton.

Everett, C., & Koerpel, B. (1986). Family therapy supervision: a review and critique of the literature. *Contemporary Family Therapy, 8* (1): 62–72.

Faris, J. (1997). "A Systemic View on the Therapist Use of Self." Unpublished paper, proceedings from the UK Council for Psychotherapy Professional Conference, Cambridge.

Flaskas, C. (1999). Limits and possibilities of postmodern narrative self. *Australian and New Zealand Journal of Family Therapy, 20* (1 March).

Flaskas, C., & Perlesz, A. (Eds.) (1996). *The Therapeutic Relationship in Systemic Therapy*. London: Karnac.

Flemons, D. (1991). *Completing Distinctions: Interweaving the Ideas of Gregory Bateson and Taoism into a Unique approach to Therapy*. London: Shambala.

Fourie, D. (1991). Family hypnotherapy, Erickson or systems? *Journal of Family Therapy* 13:1.

Freedman, J., & Combs, G. (1996). *Narrative Therapy*. New York: W. W. Norton.

Freud, S. (1895d) (with Breuer, J.). *Studies on Hysteria. The Standard Edition of the Complete Psychological Works of Sigmund Freud, Vol. 2.* London: Hogarth Press, 1955.

Friedman, M., & Jaranson, J. (1992). The applicability of the PTSD concept to refugees. In: A. J. Marsella et al. (Eds.), *Amidst Peril and Pain. The Mental Health and Social Wellbeing of the World's Refugees* (pp. 207–228). Washington, D.C., American Psychological Association.

Fruggeri, L. (1998). *Famiglie. Dinamiche interpersonali e processi psicosociali*. Rome: Carocci.

Gergen K. (1985). The social constructionist movement in modern psychology. *American Psychologist, 40*: 266–275.

Gergen, K. (1988). Knowledge and social process. In: D. Bar-Tal & A. W. Kruglanski (Eds.), *The Social Psychology of Knowledge* (pp. 30–47). Cambridge: Cambridge University Press.

Gergen, K. (1991). *The Saturated Self*. New York: Basic Books.

Gergen, K., & Kaye, J. (1992). Beyond narrative in the negotiation of therapeutic meaning. In: K. Gergen & S. McNamee (Eds.), *Therapy as Social Construction*. London: Sage.

Goderez, B. I. (1987). The survivor syndrome: massive psychic trauma and posttraumatic stress disorder. *Bulletin of the Menninger Clinic, 51*: 96–101.

Goffman, E. (1961). *Asylums: Essays on the Social Situations of Mental Patients and Other Inmates*. New York: Pelican Books.

Gorman, J. (2000). *Understanding Post-traumatic Stress Disorder*. London: Mind Publications.

Haley, J. (1963). *Strategies of Psychotherapy*. London: Grune & Stratton.

Haley, J. (1976). *Problem-Solving Therapy*. New York: Harper.

Haley, J. (1996). *Learning and Teaching Therapy*. New York: Guilford Press.

Hampton, J. (Ed). (1998). *Internally Displaced People. A Global Survey*. London: Earthscan.

Hannah, C. (1994). The context of culture in systemic therapy: an application of CMM. *Human systems, 5* (1 & 2).

Hardy, K. V., & Laszloffy, T. A. (1995). The cultural genogram: key to training culturally competent family therapists. *Journal of Marital and Family Therapy, 21*: 227–237.

Harré, R. (1989). Language games and the texts of identity. In: J. Shotter & K. Gergen (Eds.), *Texts and Identity* (pp. 20–35). London: Sage.

Harré, R., & van Langenhove, L. (1998). New directions for positioning theory. In: R. Harré (Ed.), *Positioning Theory: Moral Contexts of International Action*. Oxford: Blackwells.

Harris, Q., & Burnham, J. (1997). "Infatuation, Inspiration and Influences: An Appreciative Account of Our Relationship with the Milan Approach since 1979." Unpublished paper presented to the Conference to Celebrate 25 Years of the Milan Approach, Milan.

Hawkins, O., & Shohet, R. (1989). *Supervision in the Helping Professions: An Individual, Group and Organizational Approach*. Milton Keynes: Open University.

Healy, D. (1993). *Images of trauma. From Hysteria to Post-Traumatic Stress Disorder*. London: Faber & Faber.

Heisenberg, W. (1958). *Physics and Philosophy*. New York: Harper & Row.

Herman, J. L. (1992). *Trauma and Recovery: The Aftermath of Violence: from Domestic Abuse to Political Terror*. New York: Basic Books.

Hertz, S., & Nielsen, J. (1999). Nye dialoger i arbejdet med truede børn og deres voksne—et perspektiv om "preferred meanings". In: *Fokus på Familien, Vol. 4* (pp. 245–259). Oslo: Scandinavian University Press, Universitetsforlaget.

Hildebrand, J. (1998). *Bridging the Gap. A Training Module in Personal and Professional Development*. London: Karnac.

Hoffman, L. (1985). Beyond power and control: towards a second-order systems therapy. *Family Systems Medicine, 3*: 381–396.

Højholt, C. (1993): *Brugerperspektiver, Forældres, læreres og psykologers erfaringer med psykosocialt arbejde*, København: Dansk Psykologisk Forlag.

hooks, b. (1994). *Teaching to Transgress: Education as the Practice of Freedom*. London: Routledge.

Imber-Black, E. (1988). *Families and LArger Systems*. New York: Guilford Press.

Jackson, D. (1957). A note on the importance of trauma in the genesis of schizophrenia. *Psychiatry, 20* (2): 181–184.

Joly, D. (1996). *Haven or Hell? Asylum Policies and Refugees in Europe*. London: Macmillan.

Jones, E. (1993). *Family Systems Therapy: Developments in the Milan Systemic Therapies*. Chichester: Wiley.

Jørgensen, P. S., et al. (1993). *Risikobørn: Hvem er de—hvad gør vi?* Kbenhanv: Det tværministerielle børneudvalg, Socialministeriet.

Joseph, S., & Yule, W. (1997). *Post-Traumatic Stress Disorder. A Psychosocial Perspective and Treatment*. London: Wiley.

Kelley, P. (1994). Integrating systemic and postsystemic approaches to social work practice with refugee families. *Families in Society, 75*: 541–548.

Knowles, M. (1990). *The Adult Learner: A Neglected Species*. Houston, TX: Gulf Publishing.

Kolb, D. A. (1984). *Experiential Learning*. Englewood Cliffs, NJ: Prentice-Hall.

Krause, I.-B. (1998). *Therapy across Cultures*. London: Jessica Kingsley.

Kushner, T., & Knox, K. (1999). *Refugees in an Age of Genocide. Global, National and Local Perspectives during the Twentieth Century*. London: Frank Cass.

LaCapra, D. (2000). *Writing History, Writing Trauma*. Baltimore, MD: Johns Hopkins University Press.

Lang, W. P., Little, M., & Cronen, V. (1990). The systemic professional: domains of action and the question of neutrality. *Human Systems, 1* (1): 34–49.

Lannamann, J. W. (1991). Interpersonal communication research as ideological practice. *Communication Theory, 3*: 179–203.

Lask, B. (1998). Reflecting on mistakes and learning from experience. *Journal of Family Therapy, 2* (2).

Lau, A. (1986). Family therapy across cultures. In: *Transcultural Psychiatry* (chapter 14). London: Croom Helm.

Lau, A. (1988). Family therapy and ethnic minorities. In: E. Street & W. Dryden (Eds). *Family Therapy in Britain*. Milton Keynes: Open University Press.

Lebowitz, L., & Newman, E. (1996). The role of cognitive-affective themes in the assessment and treatment of trauma reactions. *Clinical Psychology and Psychotherapy, 3* (3): 196–207.

Lee, R. E. (1999). Developmental contextualism, isomorphism, and supervision: reflections on Roberts, Winek and Mulgrew. *Contemporary Family Therapy, 21* (3): 303–307.

Liddle, H. A., & Saba, G. W. (1983). On context replication: the isomorphic relationship of training and therapy. *Journal of Strategic and Systemic Family Therapies, 2* (2): 3–11.

Liddle, H. A., & Schwartz, R. C. (1983). Live supervision/consultation: conceptual and pragmatic guidelines for family therapy trainers. *Family Process, 22*: 477–490.

Lieberman, S. (1979). Transgenerational analysis: the genogram as a technique in family therapy. *Journal of Family Therapy, 1*: 51–64.

Lindsey, C. (1993). Family systems reconstructed in the mind of the systemic therapist. *Human Systems, 4*: 299–310.

Littlewood, R. (1992). Towards an Intercultural Therapy. In: J. Kareem & R. Littlewood (Eds.), *Intercultural Therapy: Themes, Interpretations and Practice*. Oxford: Blackwell Scientific Publications.

Loescher, G. (1993). *Beyond Charity. International Cooperation and the Global Refugee Crisis*. New York: Oxford University Press.

Marsella, A. J. (1992). Ethno-cultural diversity and the international refugee: challenges for the global community. In: A. J. Marsella et al. (Eds.), *Amidst Peril and Pain: The Mental Health and Social Wellbeing of the World's Refugees*. Washington, D.C.: American Psychological Association.

Marsella, A. J., et al. (1996). Ethnocultural aspects of PTSD: an overview of issues and research directions. In: A. J. Marsella et al. (Eds.), *Ethnocultural Aspects of Posttraumatic Stress Disorder. Issues, Research and Clinical Applications* (pp. 105–129). Washington, D.C.: American Psychological Association.

Mason, B. (1993). Towards positions of safe uncertainty. *Human Systems, 4* (Special Issue, 3 & 4): 189–200.

Mason, B. (1994). Experimenting with change: an exercise in team consultation. *Australian and New Zealand Journal of Family Therapy, 15* (2): 111–113.

Mason, B. (1999). "From Positions of 'Not Knowing' to Positions of Authoritative Doubt." Plenary address to the Australian Family Therapy Conference, Sydney, Australia (unpublished).

Masson, J. (1984). *The Assault on Truth: Freud's Suppression of the Seduction Theory*. Harmondsworth: Penguin.

Maturana, H., & Varela, F. (1980). *Autopoiesis and Cognition*. Dordrecht, Holland: Reidel.

McGoldrick, M. (1994). Culture, class, race, and gender. *Human Systems, 5*: 137–151.

McGoldrick, M., & Gerson, R. (1985). *Genograms in Family Assessments*. New York: Norton.

McGoldrick, M., Pearce. J. K., & Giordano, J. (1982). *Ethnicity and Family Therapy*. New York: Guilford Press.

Mielcke, J. (1998). *Børn på Tværs*. Frederikshavn: Dafolo.

Montgomery, J. R. (1998). Components of refugee adaptation. *International Migration Review, 30*: 679–702.

Moscovici, S. (1989). Preconditions for explanation in social psychology. *European Journal of Social Psychology, 19*: 407–430.

Muecke, M. (1992). A new paradigm for refugee health problems. *Social Science and Medicine, 35*: 515–523.

Münster, T., & Schmidt, T. (1997). Undersøgelse af familier med børn anbragt udenfor hjemmet, I. *Nordisk Psykologi, 49* (1): 68–76.

Nagera, H. (Ed.) (1970). *Basic Psychoanalytic Concepts on Metapsychology, Conflicts, Anxiety, and Other Subjects*. London: Allen & Unwin.

Nielsen, J. (1998). "Intervention og ressourceudvikling I barnets samlede netværk—en konsultativ opgave for PPR." Ålborg Symposiom, PPR, Ålborg Kommune.

Nissen, P. (1998). *Om udarbejdelse af børnepsykologiske undersøgelser*, København: Pædagogisk Psykologisk Forlag.

O'Brien, L. S. (1998). *Traumatic Events and Mental Health*. Cambridge: Cambridge University Press.

Papadopoulos, R. K. (1997). Individual identity and collective narratives of conflict. *Harvest: Journal for Jungian Studies, 43* (2): 7–26.

Papadopoulos, R. K. (1998). Destructiveness, atrocities and healing: epistemological and clinical reflections. *Journal of Analytical Psychology, 43* (4): 455–477.

Papadopoulos, R. K. (1999a). Working with families of Bosnian medical evacuees: therapeutic dilemmas. *Clinical Child Psychology and Psychiatry, 4* (1), 107–120.

Papadopoulos, R. K (1999b). Storied community as secure base: response to the paper by Nancy Caro Hollander, "Exile: Paradoxes of loss and creativity". *British Journal of Psychotherapy, 15* (3): 322–332.

Papadopoulos, R. K. (2000a). Factionalism and interethnic conflict: narratives in myth and politics. In: T. Singer (Ed.), *The Vision Thing: Myth, Politics and Psyche in the World*. London & New York: Routledge.

Papadopoulos, R. K. (2000b). A matter of shades: trauma and psychosocial work in Kosovo. In: N. Losi (Ed.), *Psychosocial and Trauma Response in War-Torn Societies: The Case of Kosovo*. Geneva: I.O.M.

Papadopoulos, R. K. (in press). Narratives of translating—interpreting with refugees: the subjugation of individual discourses. In: R. Tribe & H. Raval (Eds.), *Working with Interpreters in Mental Health*. London: Routledge.

Papadopoulos, R. K., & Hildebrand, J. (1997). Is home where the heart is? Narratives of oppositional discourses in refugee families. In: R. Papadopoulos & J. Byng-Hall (Eds.), *Multiple Voices: Narrative in Systemic Family Psychotherapy* (pp. 206–236). London: Duckworth.

Paterson, T. (1996). Leaving well alone: a systemic perspective on the therapeutic relationship. In: C. Flaskas & A. Perlesz (Eds.), *The Therapeutic Relationship in Systemic Therapy*. London: Karnac.

Pearce, B., & Cronen, V. (1980). *Communication, Action, and Meaning*. New York: Praeger.

Pearce, W. B. (1989). *Communication and the Human Condition*. Carbondale, IL: Southern Illinois University Press.

Potter, J. (1993). "Social Constructionism: Theory, Practice, Research." Plenary conference debate, Lofoten, Norway (unpublished).

Preston, R. (1999). Researching repatriation and reconstruction; who is researching what and why? In: R. Black & K. Koser (Eds.), *The End of the Refugee Cycle? Refugee Repatriation and Reconstruction*. New York: Berghahn Books.

Radovanovic, D. (1993). Prisoners of identity: a conversation with Dr Gianfranco Cecchin. *Human Systems*, *4* (1): 3–18.

Rambo, A. H. & Shilts, L. (1997). Four supervisory practices that foster respect for difference. In: T. C. Todd & C. L. Storm (Eds.), *The Complete Systemic Supervisor: Context, Philosophy, and Pragmatics*. Boston: Allyn & Bacon.

Reed, A. (1993). The reflecting team in a systemic therapy training context. *Human Systems*,*4*: 213–229.

Reichelt, S., & Sveaass, N. (1994). Therapy with refugee families: what is a "good" conversation? *Family Process*, *33*: 247–262.

Rober, P. (1999). The therapist's inner conversation in family therapy practice: some ideas about the self of the therapist, therapeutic impasse, and the process of reflection. *Family Process*, *38*: 209–228.

Roberts, J. (1989). Training with O (observing) and T (treatment): teams in live supervision: reflections in the looking glass. *Journal of Marital and Family Therapy*, *15*: 397–410.

Roberts, T. W., Winek, J., & Mulgrew, J. (1999). A systems/dialectical model of supervision: a symbolic process. *Contemporary Family Therapy*, *21* (3): 291–301.

Roper-Hall, A. (1997). Working systemically with older people and their families who "have come to grief". In: P. Sutcliffe, G. Tufnell, & U. Cornish (Eds.), *Working with the Dying and Bereaved*. London. Macmillan.

Royal College of Psychiatrists (1998). *Focus on Clinical Audit in Child and Adolescent Mental Health Services*. Dorchester: Ling.

Scaife, J. (1993). Setting the scene for supervision. *Human Systems, 4*: 161–172.

Schön, D. (1983). *The Reflective Practitioner: How Professionals Think in Action*. New York: Basic Books.

Schön, D. (1987). *Educating the Reflective Practitioner*. San Francisco, CA: Jossey Bass.

Scott, M., & Palmer, S. (1999). *Trauma and Post-Traumatic Stress Disorder: Stress Counselling*. London: Continuum.

Selvini Palazzoli, M. S., Boscolo, L., Cecchin, G., & Prata, G. (1980). Hypothesizing, circularity and neutrality: three guidelines for the conductor of the session. *Family Process, 19* (1): 3–12.

Shamai, M. (1998). Therapist in distress: team-supervision of social workers and family therapists who work and live under political uncertainty. *Family Process, 37*: 245–259.

Shephard, B. (2000). *A War of Nerves: Soldiers and Psychiatrists 1914–1994*. London: Cape.

Shotter, J. (1990). *Knowing of the Third Kind*. Utrecht: ISOR/University of Utrecht.

Sprenkle, D. H. (1999). Toward a general model of family therapy supervision: comment on Roberts, Winek and Mulgrew. *Contemporary Family Therapy, 21* (3): 309–315.

Sprenkle, D. H., & Moon, S. M. (1996). *Research Methods in Family Therapy*. New York. Guilford Press.

Storm, C. L., & Haug, I. E. (1997). Ethical issues. Where do you draw the line? In: T. C. Todd & C. L. Storm (Eds.), *The Complete Systemic Supervisor: Context, Philosophy, and Pragmatics* (pp. 26–40). London: Allyn & Bacon.

Storm, C. L., et al. (1997). Supervisory Challenge 12: evaluating supervision. In: C. L. Storm & T. C. Todd (Eds.), *The Reasonably Complete Systemic Supervisor Resource Guide* (pp. 180–208). London: Allyn & Bacon.

Stratton, P. (1998). Culture in systemic practice. *Human Systems*, 9 (3–4): 155–158.

Summerfield, D. (1999). A critique of seven assumptions behind psychological trauma programmes in war-affected areas. *Social Sciences and Medicine*, 48: 1449–1462.

Summerfield, D. (2001). The invention of post-traumatic stress disorder and the social usefulness of a psychiatric category. *British Medical Journal, 322* (13 January): 95–98.

Tedeschi, R. G., & Calhoun, L. G. (1995). *Trauma and Transformation: Growing in the Aftermath of Suffering*. New York: Sage.

Thompson Drewal, M. (1992). *Yoruba Ritual: Performers, Play, Agency*. Bloomington, IN: Indiana University Press.

Tomm, K., "Cynthia", "Andrew" and "Vanessa" (1992). Therapeutic distinctions in an on-going therapy. In: S. McNamee & K. J. Gergen (Eds.), *Therapy as Social Construction* (pp. 116–135). London: Sage.

Uggerhøj, L. (1995). *Hjælp eller afhængighed*. Aalborg: Aalborg Universitetsforlag.

Ursano, R. J., & McCaughey, B. G. (1995). *Individual and Community Responses to Trauma and Disaster. The Structure of Human Chaos*. Cambridge: Cambridge University Press.

Varela, F. (1979). *Principles of Biological Autonomy*. New York: North Holland.

Veer, G. van der (1994). *Counselling and Therapy with Refugees: Psychological Problems of Victims of War, Torture and Repression*. Chichester: Wiley.

Vernez, G. (1991). Current global refugee situation and international public policy. *American Psychologist, 46*: 627–631.

Von Foerster, H. (1981). *Observing Systems*. Seaside, CA: Intersystems Publications.

Von Foerster, H. (1990). "Ethics and Second-Order Cybernetics." Paper given at the International Conference on Systems and Family Therapy—Ethics, Epistemology, New Methods. Paris (unpublished).

von Glasersfeld, E. (1984). An introduction to radical constructivism. In: P. Watzlawick (Ed.), *The Invented Reality* (pp. 17–40). New York: Norton.

Watts, A. (1975). *Tao: The Watercourse Way*. New York: Pantheon Books.

Watzlawick, P., Beavin, J., & Jackson, D. D. (1967). *Pragmatics of Human Communication*. New York: Norton.

Watzlawick, P., Weakland, J., & Fisch, R. (1974). *Change: Principles of Problem Formation and Problem Resolution*. New York: Norton.

Weiner-Davis, M., de Shazer, S., & Gingerich, W. J. (1987). Building on pre-treatment change to construct the therapeutic solution: an exploratory study. *Journal of Marital and Family Therapy, 13*: 359–365.

White, M. (1997). *Narratives of Therapists' Lives.* Adelaide: Dulwich Centre Publications.

Wieling, E., & Marshall, J. P. (1999). Cross-cultural supervision in marriage and family therapy. *Contemporary Family Therapy, 21* (3): 317–329.

Wilson, J. (1993). The supervisory relationship in family therapy training. *Human Systems, 4*: 173–187.

Woodcock, J (1994). Family therapy with refugees and political exiles. *Context, 20*: 37–41.

Yehuda, R., & McFarlane, A. C. (1995). Conflict between current knowledge about posttraumatic stress disorder and its original conceptual basis. *Trauma Information Pages* (Internet publication): www.trauma-pages.com/yehuda95.htm.

Young, A. (1997). *The Harmony of Illusions. Inventing Post-Traumatic Stress Disorder.* Princeton, NJ: Princeton University Press.

Yule, W. (1999). *Post-Traumatic Stress Disorder. Concepts and Therapy.* London: Wiley.

Zur, J. (1996). From PTSD to voices in context: from an "experience-far" to "experience-near" understanding of responses to war and atrocity across cultures. *International Journal of Social Psychiatry, 42*: 305–317.

INDEX